LOUISIANA PLANTATION HOMES

HOMES

[**COLONIAL AND ANTEBELLUM**]

BY W. DARRELL OVERDYKE

AMERICAN LEGACY PRESS • NEW YORK

OPENING PAGE: *The entrance door to Parlange, one of the oldest plantations in the state, has warmly welcomed visitors for two centuries*

FRONTISPIECE: *The tall columns of Woodlawn were the products of the lush sugar-land slave economy doomed by the Civil War.*

PHOTO CREDITS

Milburne Alfred, 177
Ernestine M. Brown, 27
William Grabill, 201
Frances Benjamin Johnston, 46, 47, 48, 102, 105 bot., 120, 121, 132, 133, 163, 167 top, 170, 178, 191, 192, 194, 196, 197, 198, 202, 205
Lester Jones, 70, 71 top, 103, 105 top, 111

Richard Koch, 31, 40, 41, 49, 50, 71 bot., 116, 117, 149, 154, 155, 160, 161, 168, 169, 188, 207, 208
Charles E. Peterson, 113
Thurman C. Smith, 21, 22, 23, 24, 35, 52, 56, 77, 87, 88, 149, 174, 175, 176, 177 (R), 179, 180, 181, 182, 183, 184
Thomas T. Waterman, 51
H. O. Wiseman, 30, 59, 60, 61, 110, 138, 148

Copyright © MCMLXV by W. Darrell Overdyke
All rights reserved.

This edition is published by American Legacy Press,
distributed by Crown Publishers, Inc.,
by arrangement with Architectural Book Publishing Co.
American Legacy Press is a trademark of Crown Publishers, Inc.
h g f e d c b a
1981 EDITION

Manufactured in the United States of America

Library of Congress Cataloging in Publication Data

Overdyke, W. Darrell (William Darrell)
  Louisiana plantation homes, colonial and antebellum.

  Reprint. Originally published: New York : Architectural Book Pub. Co., 1965.
  1. Plantations—Louisiana.   2. Architecture, Colonial —Louisiana.   3. Architecture, Modern—19th century—Louisiana.   4. Eclecticism in architecture—Louisiana.
I. Title.
NA7235.L809 1981   728.8′3′09763   81-12859
ISBN 0-517-36053-5   AACR2

CONTENTS

PREFACE

For three decades with the constant and enthusiatic aid of my wife, Martha Walker Overdyke, I have gathered photographic, architectural and historic information on the homes of Louisiana. Legal records, government documents, diaries, letters, newspapers, secondary monographs of many varieties, along with oral recollections and accounts, have provided fertile sources. The recognition and appreciation of many courtesies, due several hundreds of people, cannot be adequately expressed here. The legal firm of Wade and Wade of St. Joseph, without letters of introduction, placed the records of their abstract firm at the author's disposal, including the combinations of the vaults so that research could be conducted over the week-end. In midafternoon on a back-country road, twenty miles or more from any eating place, a Louisiana lady prepared lunch for two hungry strangers. A middle-aged man, in response to request for directions, said, "Follow me, it's only ten miles out of my way," and then led the way through a maze of winding back-country roads. On a hot August afternoon two white-headed gentlemen helped us dig the car out of a sand trap. A few years later, in December, a colored gentleman rescued us from the black mud of his sweet-potato farm. Whether white or colored, homes were opened without appointment, and measurements were permitted to be taken from the attic through every room. Students, elderly people in their nineties, Librarians of Centenary College and the Library of Congress, museums, professional architects such as Samuel Wilson, Jr., owners of homes and many others should be named. Lack of specific recognition does not lessen the sincere obligation to, and an appreciation of, those not named. Grants from the Frank Hemenway Foundation and the Carnegie Foundations were helpful. The professional photographers whose photography and processing of film were of special importance were Milburne Alfred, Clell Baker, Thurman C. Smith and H. O. Wiseman. Illustrations not otherwise accredited are those of the author. The photography of others, often taken before neglect, destruction, growth of concealing shrubbery or "restoration," has been freely used with proper accreditation. The artistry of one of America's greatest architectural photographers, Miss Frances Benjamin Johnston, is but one example.

In no sense is this volume a guide book. All homes are private and are not open to the public unless public signs or the nature of the ownership indicates that visitors are welcome. Over the decades the changes in ownership open or close some of these homes. Current guide books and local inquiry and public signs are sometimes unreliable. Some of these houses can be seen from the public roads, as many were originally built to be viewed from the passing steamboats. Some indication of the locations is included, as the ecology, the terrain, the climate, the waterways, as well as the history, give guidance to the understanding of the unique nuances of Louisiana plantation architecture. Mere indication of parish (county) or adjunct small town is not always sufficient. Therefore a variety of methods is used.

ARKANSAS

TEXAS

MISSIS

ALEXANDER

BLAKEMORE

STAR ARLINGTON

BUENA VISTA

ROSENEATH

LANDS END

BERMUDA

WAVERTREE

MELROSE

BROWNELL

LLOYD HALL

ELLERSLIE

PARLANGE

CHRÉTIEN POINT

ARLINGTON

NOTTAWAY

Burnside

SHADOWS-ON-THE-TECHE

MADEWOOD

Tensas

CASS
MILLER TLAFAYETTE TCOLUMBIA I UNION
CADDO
MARION
BOSSIER WEBSTER
CLAIBORNE
UNION
ASHLEY
CHICOT
WASHINGTON
ISSAQUE
MOREHOUSE
WEST CARROLL
EAST CARROLL
HARRISON
LINCOLN
PANOLA
OUACHITA
RICHLAND
MADISON
DE SOTO
BIENVILLE
JACKSON
RED RIVER
CALDWELL
FRANKLIN
SHELBY
WINN
SABINE
NATCHITOCHES
LA SALLE
CATAHOULA
CLAIBO
JEFFERSON
CONCORDIA
SABINE
GRANT
ADAMS
RAPIDES
AVOYELLES
VERNON
WILKINSON
NEWTON
POINTE COUPEE
WEST FELICIANA
EAST FELICIA
BEAUREGARD
ALLEN
EVANGELINE
SAINT LANDRY
EAST BATON ROUG
CALCASIEU
JEFFERSON DAVIS
ACADIA
SAINT MARTIN
IBERVILLE
WEST BATON ROUGE
ORANGE
LAFA
CAMERON
VERMILION
IBERIA
SAINT MARY
PART OF ST MARTIN
ASSUMPTION
JEFFERSON

Copyright by RAND McNALLY & COMPANY, R. L. 65Y64

LOUISIANA PLANTATION HOMES

[COLONIAL AND ANTEBELLUM]

BY W. DARRELL OVERDYKE

WALTHALL   MARION

KE   GIPAHOA WASHINGTON   PEARL RIVER

SAINT TAMMANY

HANCOCK

JOHN BAPTIST

SAN FRANCISCO   SPANISH CUSTOM HOUSE

SAINT CHARLES   ORLEANS

ORMOND   SAINT BERNARD   BUENO RETIRO

JEFFERSON   PLAQUEMINES

MARY   ORANGE GROVE

MAGNOLIA

SCALE IN MILES
0 5 10   20   30   40

LOUISIANA PARISHES
Total Number 64
1960 Populations

INTRODUCTION

Oh won't you come along with me
To the Mississippi?
We'll take a boat to the land of dreams,
Steam down the river, down to New Orleans.

TRADITION, the movies, jazz and popular music have created a stereotype in the American mind about Louisiana, and especially about New Orleans on the Mississippi. Some of the legend is valid and can be savored readily enough by today's visitor. Whether he visits the Vieux Carré and its famous restaurants in person, by travelogue or by the printed page, he will enjoy his most exhilarating experiences only when he sees the other parts of Louisiana. Truly, going down the Mississippi takes one into a land of dreams, a heaven on earth. But New Orleans is only a faint foretaste of the shifting, changing, ever more intriguing Louisiana found in the state's bayous, rivers, lakes, swamps, hills and prairies — the backdrops of its history.

Romantic, nostalgic, sad, happy, fanciful — but real and tangible — the past still lives, picturesquely and abundantly. Everywhere in the state, the sensitive observer who gets away from the shopping centers a few miles, or even a few blocks, finds himself slipping into bygone eras. Spanish, French and English colonizers all have left indelible legacies, racial, cultural and linguistic as well as physical.

This book is concerned primarily with the colonial and plantation residences of the flush period that preceded the Civil War. An introductory historical-background sketch offers a foundation for fuller appreciation of the charm and beauty of these homes.

Several factors combine to make Louisiana unique in the United States. Its location and climate, its people and history have produced ways of life and living found nowhere else in our country. During the colonial period, settlers came from Spain, France and England. Negro slaves arrived in large numbers. The native Indian population was small.

The Spanish were the earliest explorers, some 200 years before the French; but the French made the first actual colonization, at the end of the seventeenth century. Political sovereignty shifted to Spain in 1763, but the Louisiana French maintained their dominance in language and continued their softer, more easy-going way of life in social relations and religion.

Until good roads, radios and compulsory public education brought their changes during the 1920s and 1930s, English was seldom used by the country folk in many parts of the state. There are still areas today where children starting in school cannot speak English.

Except for the exuberant, roistering aggressive Americans, the southern-Louisiana Creole has displayed a remarkable ability to assimilate and "Creolize" all newcomers. In the decade before the Civil War, large numbers of German and Irish immigrants were successfully absorbed, their surnames gallicized.

In Louisiana today the word Creole has no legal significance. The Alabama Supreme Court has held that to be a Creole is to be a Negro, but this is not so in Louisiana. Originally the term Creole, in the rigid legal classification of the Spanish Colonial Code of the Indies, meant any person, regardless of rank or wealth, born in the New World of pure European parentage. Today it means an inheritance and a way of life. It may be used as an adjective—Creole gumbo, Creole pralines, Creole lilies, etc. A Creole Negro would be a Negro reared in a Creole section, speaking French — but he would not be a Creole.

"Cajun" — a corruption of "Acadian," — was the term applied to the country-cousin, "swampbilly" Creoles who settled along the interior bayous. A bayou is, generally speaking, a slow-moving, meandering stream, usually draining into swampy cypress bottom lands.

To gain a complete empathy for Louisianans as they have lived in the 1800s, and even in the twentieth century, to achieve a sense of communication, to feel as if one were an inhabitant, one must become accommodated to the slow, languorous tempo that has permeated their life. A modern American finds it difficult to orient himself to an environment in which events follow a slow, gradual, seldom-varied sequence. It is even more difficult for a non-Southerner to visualize a land where one season merges into the next with little change in temperature or rainfall or vegetation. It is as though men, animals, plants have reached a harmonious accommodation with prolonged heat and copious moisture. Thus man and beast have been able to live longer; and in former days the incredible richness of the well watered soil meant opulence for the large plantation owners, and more than a sufficiency for others.

Except for "the City" (New Orleans) and a few small inland towns, Louisiana was completely rural before 1860. Rural isolation and the slowness of travel, almost always by water, fostered a closeness of family life and family relationships that was cherished and preserved. A plantation home was the focus of all social and economic activities. Louisiana homes were built to be born in, to live in, to marry in, to die in and to provide a haven for the entertainment of friends and relatives. They were built for comfort, to accord with the prevailing weather. And they were built for show. Outside of fine carriages and horses, a splurge in New Orleans or a European Grand Tour, what else could a gentleman use his money for? His table could vary but little from that of his neighbor, or from that of his slaves. He could add wine, a few imported delicacies, sumptuous service — that was about all. His main extravagance was his home and its furnishings.

A Louisiana builder, be he rich, fairly prosperous or poor, could with little effort find a luxurious natural setting amid an almost semi-tropical lushness to enrich his home. Whether it was a typical Creole house, an Anglo-Saxon dogtrot log cabin, an expanse of ornamental ironwork or a Greek Revival mansion with gleaming white columns, the extravagantly verdant Louisiana background complemented it.

There are two natural, dominant, unvarying colors in Louisiana's landscape, the year round. The first is the dull, unbelievable grayness of the swampy regions, only partially sensed by the tourists who race along the highways. The second is a continuous greenness: there is seldom a day — from the colder northern parishes to the shores of the Gulf — that a glance does not take in a lavish display of green trees and shrubs and blooming flowers. If for no other reason than this, a Louisiana plantation home set down on a New England hilltop, or on Ohio flat land, would not be the same esthetically. It might be as attractive, conceivably, but its quality would be entirely different.

Louisiana is South: Deep South-plus — the plus being humidity. Its rainfall is one of the highest in the nation. Lakes and bayous are numerous. The Mississippi, the Red River of the South and other sizeable streams add to the moisture content of the region. Except during flood time, when the waters of the land from the Rockies on the west to the Appalachians on the east and to the Great Lakes on the north, pour down through the state, Louisiana's rivers flow slowly. Rivers, lakes and bayous, the wide swamps, the Gulf of Mexico — all contribute their moisture to make the state's humidity.

The growing season is long. The southernmost parishes are so frost free that oranges are grown commercially. Sugar cane is planted as far north as the upper third of the state. Citrus, sugar cane, rice, figs, sweet potatoes, palms, year-round vegetable and flower gardens indicate the warm climate.

The state's topography varies widely, with two extremes: the hill lands stand in contrast to the river-bottom and delta lands and the swamps behind them. Hills are found in the Florida Parishes, north and east of Baton Rouge; in northern Louisiana, cut through by the Red and Ouachita rivers and their tributaries; and in the western section bordering on Texas. Very few of these hill lands attain a height of more than 300 feet.

The soil of the hill lands is generally poor. That of the deltas and the low swamps behind the rivers is fabulously rich. There the top soil is often as deep as a man can dig, so rich that new slave plantations never needed fertilizers. Elevations in the extreme southern Gulf Parishes are only a few feet above sea level.

In the western Gulf Parishes, the prairie extended from Opelousas to

Lake Charles. Here the first American cowboy faced problems different from those of the cowboy later portrayed so widely on movie and television screens. It was not desert and thirst that endangered the Louisiana ranch hand, but bog and too much water. The large plantations on these prairies grow sugar cane, rice and cotton.

The rivers and lesser waterways — natural, practicable highways — were the early settlers' routes for getting their farm and forest products to market. The highways that interlace the state today touch relatively few corners that were not formerly accessible by steamboat or pirogue. Water transportation has not yet been supplanted. More tonnage is carried on Louisiana's multitudinous waterways today than ever before.

The oldest and the most elegant homes were found near the streams because of dependence on water communication and the fertility of the soil in these areas. The rivers gave wealth; they also destroyed — floods and changes in river beds have taken a heavy toll of plantation homes. During the Civil War, Union armies moved throughout the state by river gunboat and transport. Pillaging and wanton destruction damaged or ruined many fine town and plantation homes.

Not all the wartime destruction was wrought by the Yankees. One of the most sumptuous residences in the northern Louisiana Mississippi River delta was burned down by its Confederate owner. When the Federal gunboats ran the Vicksburg blockade, he told the Union officers quartered on his place they would not sleep another night in his house, set fire to it and returned to his native England.

Louisiana's history is old — older than that of New England or the Atlantic coastal states. After the discovery of the New World the Spanish early launched exploring parties from their Caribbean outposts. Alonzo de Pineda sailed along the Louisiana coast in 1519. Nine years later, another and larger expedition, led by Panfilo de Narvaez and Cabeza de Vaca, was stranded in Florida. Painfully they made their way on foot along the Gulf coast, trying to reach Hernando Cortez' Spanish Mexico. Indians captured and enslaved the expedition's remnants on the Louisiana-Texas coast.

Cabeza de Vaca managed to win semi-freedom for himself as an Indian trader roaming far into the interior. Eight years later, by way of Mexico, he returned to Spain. His report to the Spanish King, which was widely published in many languages, included descriptions of the land and people of Louisiana.

A few years later Hernando de Soto led an even more ambitious expedition to Florida. After landing and struggling through much of the present southeast United States, De Soto died and was buried near the Red River. While De Soto was vainly searching for gold in the southeast, Francisco Coronado was doing the same in the southwest. With no gold discovered and few Indians found to enslave and Christianize, Spain showed little interest in colonizing the great river-basin territory, and adopted a keep-out, dog-in-the-manger policy.

A century later, the French pushed up the St. Lawrence River to reach the Great Lakes. Hearing of the mighty Mississippi, they moved west and south. In the face of many obstacles, the intrepid Sieur de la Salle reached the mouth of the great river in the spring of 1682 and claimed for France the territory drained by its waters, naming it Louisiana, the land of Louis.

Later he returned to France and embarked with four ships and colonists to settle Louisiana. Sailing too far west, he and his colonists were marooned on a desolate stretch of the Gulf Coast, where they met violent death. In 1698 more French settlers, led by Iberville and Bienville, made a landing on the sandy Mississippi coast. Later they were moved to Alabama.

In 1714 the French established the first colony in the Mississippi Valley, in what is now the state of Louisiana. Located on the Red River at Natchitoches, this was a western post to hold back the Spaniards. Immediately the Spanish moved north from Mexico to place a mission and military post at Los Adaes, a few miles west of Natchitoches. In 1716 the French set up an eastern post, at what is now Natchez, Mississippi, to deter the British. New Orleans was laid out in 1718, and in 1722 it became the capital of French Louisiana.

In 1763, with the British finally victorious in their long conflict against the French in North America, Louisiana Territory was divided between England and Spain. All of it east of the Mississippi, except the Isle of Orleans, went to the British. All of it west of the great river, plus New Orleans, went to Spain. The eastern part of the present state of Louisiana, including Baton Rouge, remained in British hands to the end of the Revolutionary War. Then it was transferred to Spain, and remained under Spanish rule even after the Louisiana Purchase, 1803. It was still Spanish when Louisiana became a state in 1812, but with the purchase of Florida by the United States in 1819 the West Florida Parishes (in eastern Louisiana) were acquired.

This shifting of control or sovereignty among Spain, France, England and the United States — not to mention brief periods of independence (after rebellions in 1810 and 1812, in the Florida Parishes, and after secession and prior to the formation of the Confederacy, in the whole state) — helps to explain the diversification of the colonists and their descendants. Cultural, economic, religious and racial differences, as well as peculiar geographical factors, have had their effects not only on the state's inhabitants but on the styles of its architecture.

It has been pointed out that the widely used term "Southern Colonial Style" is a misnomer since only the Carolinas, Virginia, Georgia, Louisiana, with perhaps a small strip of Alabama and Mississippi were ever colonial. Kentucky, Tennessee, Alabama, Mississippi, Arkansas and Missouri had little or no colonial background. Louisiana as a colony of three different nations developed its own distinctive architecture and made important original contributions to the architectural heritage of America. Individuality is easily discernible in terms of design, appearance, climatic adaptability and particularly in the use of indigenous building materials.

Characteristically different were the broad verandas (galleries) giving shade to the windows and walls and providing comfortable outdoor living space. With moderate need for heating facilities, there was but slight architectural emphasis on chimneys, which were in such prominence in many colonial homes from Virginia northward.

Since winters were short and summers long and hot, Louisianians made extensive use of windows. Tall windows extended to the floor. Windows and doors often were used interchangeably.

High waters and frequent floods were an ever present menace in the state's lowlands. The Indians in ages past had solved the problem by building huge earth mounds for their villages. Creoles evolved a lower (raised basement) story of solid construction topped by a story or a story and a half as the main living quarters. Underground basements or cellars were seldom used because of high water tables and the warm climate.

To the eye, the first impression of early Louisiana Creole architecture is not necessarily the accentuated height of the steep hipped roofs, since shrubbery generally reduces this effect. The roof slopes usually continue without a break to cover the verandas. These galleries extend across the front and often down each side. The setting of Creole houses is in contrast to the formal, clipped, restrained landscaping of many New England and Southeastern homes. Most Louisiana plantations were surrounded by blooming shrubs, flowering magnolia trees, and approaches through cedars, magnolias or live oaks. In the hill lands of North Louisiana crepe myrtles and cedars were used. Ostentatious and extremely formal gardens surrounded many of the later Greek Revival homes. Alexander Porter laid out a seventy-acre park for his Bayou Teche residence. Much of this he landscaped with flowing waters, bridges and garden houses. Tasteful and expensive statuary was brought back from Europe by the cultured and wealthy planters. French gardeners were induced to lay out what were in some instances grandiose formal gardens. Grottoes, garçonnières, artificial streams, mazes, green houses, unusual vistas, and every device that ingenuity, money and a plentiful supply of plantation labor could provide, were skillfully executed. Imported trees, shrubs, flowers, rare tropicals and Asiatics were planted.

Unfortunately gardens were the first to feel the effects of reduced income. When homes were unlived in, marble paths, bricked drives, statuary were carried away or disintegrated.

The colonial and early nineteenth-century homes were purely Louisianian in materials of construction and architectural concept. When the Englishman of the original colonies built, except for the frontier log cabin and its adaptations, he tended to follow along transplanted English lines. Not so the French and Spanish in Louisiana. They created their own indigenous style. Under the Spanish there was perhaps some borrowing from the West Indian and African types, although this is controversial.

Early Creole homes, regardless of their pretensions, made use of available native building materials. Practically speaking, there was no building stone in the state. Wood, clay mixed with Spanish moss or deer hair, and — near the coast sections — tabby plaster made of shell were available. The typical frontier log cabin never appealed to the Creole.

The prevalent construction procedure was to erect a framework of hand-hewn timbers of cypress arranged in vertical angles extending from the sills to the ceiling plates. Mud mixed with moss was packed between these posts (*bousillage entre poteaux*) and allowed to harden. The early Creole could not make enduring brick. When their soft bricks were placed between the hewn framework (*briquette entre poteaux*) the walls had to be plastered or sided over. Later, when more durable bricks were produced, the plastering, often tinted, was continued. These post-and-mud walls became cementlike as the decades passed. As they were occasionally nearly two feet in thickness, they have hampered modern electricians and plumbers in renovating projects.

The lumber used is of special interest, particularly the quantities of cypress. This wood defies water and rotting. Modern lumbermen regularly dig up cypress trees deposited centuries ago in the Atchafalaya swamps under many feet of mud and mire. In Iberia Parish a farmer drilling for water who hits a deeply buried cypress has to move to a different spot so his well can be completed. Oil drills go through cypress, still solid, buried hundreds of feet underground.

Cypress cut from trees several thousands of years old made sills and building timbers. Most houses were shingled with cypress. The beauty of color and of grain of cypress boards, without paint for decades, is pleasurable to experience.

The forests of the state were replete with many varieties of oaks and pines. Hard-heart pine was used for heavy framing, pine and cypress for floors and trim. In the Feliciana Parishes, walnut, poplar and pecan woods were plentiful. The size of timbers hewn out was immense. Heart sills of log houses were sixty feet long and twenty-four or more inches square! Wavertree's rafters, built to hold an imported slate roof, are many times the size of the sills used by builders to support modern-day residences. Dovetailed, morticed and tenoned, lapped and pegged, these houses were built to last.

Termites, the bane of modern home owners, never seem to touch the old homes, but fire and flood are no respecters of age or beauty. Lack of paint, gangling shutters, boarded-up windows, sagging gutters, vines, weeds, fallen bricks or broken railings are not yet fatal signs. The menacing weaknesses of any old building seem to lie in two places, the roof and the foundation. When rain, wind and neglect make an opening, decay and eventual disaster follow. Add to these fire and flood, and many an epitaph has been written.

Several decades ago Natchez had numerous rundown mansions, many built as town residences for Louisiana planters. Today these are more spic and span, more heavily painted and neatly trimmed, and more crammed with antiques than their original owners could have conceived. Unfortunately a number of Louisiana plantation houses have lacked this refurbishing. The eye and imagination must reclothe them in their original charm.

While the older sections of Natchitoches and New Orleans are still replete with beautiful ornate Spanish and post-Spanish ironwork, the plantation homes usually utilized wood. The early Creoles might use Spanish-type iron hinges, even in plain buildings, while the Americans in the northern parishes made do with wooden hinges. Just before the Civil War much building hardware came to Louisiana from Cincinnati, Philadelphia and St. Louis. Some iron "columns" were placed on city business fronts, but only rarely was metal employed on plantation homes until the decade before the Civil War. Some cast iron was ordered from Europe. Brick or mud, and timber built the plantation home, with cut nails and pegs for the main structure. Hinges, door knobs and locks were brought in from the North or imported from Europe, of iron, brass and even of silver and gold. Copper was used for gutters in more expensive mansions and in at least one case for roofing. Newfangled galvanized roofing was commercially used but not until modern times has it replaced the original cypress shingles on some of the older but moderate-size plantation homes. Occasionally slate roofs were imported. A present-day annoying defacement, which of course could not have been on the original residences, has come with the extensive use of wire screen.

It was a rare exception for a plantation home to have running water, although Orange Grove had running hot water. Betty lamps and whale-oil lamps were seldom found. Candlelight and, for the slave, firelight were sufficient. Modern plumbing and sewerage were rare city conveniences.

Several phases of Louisiana architecture can be roughly dated. Unlike other sections of the United States the log cabin did not enter the first phase of settlement. The original colonists did not build this permanently. It was not until the migration of English-speaking stock from South Carolina, Alabama and Georgia into North Louisiana after 1830 that the log cabin was to become common. Scores of these are still inhabited, although some are not recognizable as primitive log construction.

The first homes which were more than crude temporary shelters took the Creole form of mud and posts with wide hipped roofs. These, with high raised basements often incorporating stairs inside the gallery to the main floor, were numerous in the Natchitoches and South Louisiana sections. They were built until the last quarter of the nineteenth century.

The expanding numbers of Americans in the state after its admission to the Union in 1812 coincided with the ever increasing demand for cotton. Incredibly rich lands and great numbers of slave laborers brought quick and fabulous fortunes to large planters. When cotton prices fluctuated downward a change to sugar cane assured continued wealth. As planters prospered they built new and larger homes, following generally the new trend toward Greek Revival. Some of strong Anglo-Saxon background chose the Georgian style, others amalgamated with the Louisiana patterns. The Georgian influence in the Creole sections was largely confined to refinement and elaboration of window and door details.

Few, if any, builders from 1820 to 1860 were slavish copyists of the classical modes. Southerners, and Louisianians in particular, knew the Greek Classical Revival styles from their own European travels and contacts. They were intrigued with the possibilities offered by great white columns rising to massive entablatures, and with classical façades and porticos. Yet all in all, concludes J. Frazer Smith in his *White Pillars*, Southern architecture should not be called Greek Revival. He finds Greek influence mainly in the various orders (columns) and moldings, and these emerge as definitely different forms. He believes that Gothic influences were similarly attenuated.

Tasteful modifications reveal Louisiana colonial influence in both large and small dwellings. Houses were designed and construction supervised by professional "architects," native and foreign; and by contractors, who, using standard treatises on architecture, adapted form, size and detail to suit the tastes of the owners.

The title "architect" is difficult to define. Anyone could assume it, few did. Formal accrediting agencies were nonexistent. Louisiana practitioners of the art of architecture — and there were a number of self-made competent ones — did not advertise in the New Orleans and Baton Rouge newspapers. "Master Builders" had cards inserted. The modern professional terminology was seldom used in Louisiana plantation building. When architects are known they are identified with individual construction. A number of architectural handbooks were available and used, but never slavishly. Scaled drawings for plantation buildings have not survived.

Eclecticism was applied to all forms and modes. Louisianians developed their own tasteful and gracious styles which differed from those of any other state. They did not conform to the snobbish narrow concept of a way of life that guided all American construction, as Wayne Andrews indicates in his volume, *Architecture, Ambitions and Americans*.

The contractors often owned or hired highly skilled and highly priced slaves. These, with a few white mechanics and the planter's own unskilled slave labor, molded the brick, formed the lumber, built the house, its doors, windows, its panels, wainscots and its trim inside and out. In the final decade of the ante-bellum period the steam mills of New Orleans and St. Louis supplied imposing millwork for windows, doors, stairways and inside trim in a wide variety of styles. Thus the builder could individualize his house, even beyond the skills of the particular artisans he was using. Mansions were, particularly in the later years, fitted with imported iron or marble mantels. Some plaster cornices, frieze work, moldings, rosettes, stair rails and carvings were done by local or transient artisans. Much came directly from Europe.

Boykin Witherspoon, owning 151 slaves and 5500 acres of land, started a two-year house construction in the northern parish of De Soto. His contract was general in nature.

State of Louisiana, Parish of DeSoto
Nov th 29 1859

Memorandum of an agreement or contract this day made & entered into between M. Robbins of the one part & Boykin Witherspoon of the other part (both citizens domicitited in the State & Parish above written). Witnesseth that the said Robbins on his part agrees and binds himself to do the carpenters work in a workman like manner according to such plan and specifications as said Witherspoon may furnish or desire, the said Witherspoon on his part obligating himself to pay said Robbins one hundred dollars per month together with board & lodging for himself & horse and to pay monthly for the hands now in the employment of said Robbins or such of them as he may wish to keep, the same wages as he may have to pay to the owners of said hands. The said Witherspoon having the right to put such of his own negroes as he may wish to work on said house under the direction & control of said Robbins.

Witness: B. Witherspoon
C. A. Edwards   M. Robbins

Robbins had in his library the standard architectural works, including Lafevere, and Brown and Jay. According to the contract, Witherspoon was to supply the plans, though it was more than likely that Robbins did so and merely made modifications according to the owner's desires. Robbins built a number of large houses in the vicinity and all of these reflect his own architectural patterns. Robbins' crew included eleven Negroes whose masters received from twelve to forty dollars a month in hire. In addition to these skilled laborers, Witherspoon also furnished a force of his own hands. The plaster work was subcontracted, the lumber, except some large timbers, was steam milled, and the stair railing was purchased in New Orleans. A partial bill of materials included:

82,100 feet Lumber $ 1 pr hundred	821.00
Carpenters work	2200.00
30,000 Shingles $ 5 pr M	150.00
80,000 Brick & Laying of Same	960.00
1127 yds Plastering	1100.00
Painting, Paint & Glass	1000.00
Hardware & Nails	380.00
Spouting & Conductors	60.00
Hauling	225.00
	$6898.00

A number of plantation homes do not conform at all to either Creole or Classical mode. Of frame, plaster, brick, or of combinations in accordance with their builder's whims, they make striking and arresting contrasts to the general pattern.

Magnolia (Plaquemines Parish) built by two English sea captains before 1800 with its thick brick walls and individual lower-floor plan and Orange Grove, a typical English manor house, are examples found on the Mississippi below New Orleans. Gossypia, in the state's northeast corner, bears the air of a Mediterranean villa; while Afton Villa in West Feliciana Parish used strongly eclectic façades. Scattered over the state, particularly in the non-Creole sections, are scores of post-Federal or conventional cottage designs.

W. DARRELL OVERDYKE

ACADIAN HOUSE

The most romantic plantation home in the state, now the Acadian House Museum, was built before the American Revolution by a refugee from the former French Canadian province of Acadia, then British Nova Scotia. Henry Wadsworth Longfellow tells how Evangeline (Emmeline Labiche), forcefully separated from her betrothed Gabriel (Louis Arceneaux), wandered for years before she found her long lost lover in the deep bayou country of south Louisiana, already married. In the churchyard of St. Martinville a beautiful marker stands over Evangeline's grave. Whether half truth or legend, the Louis Arceneaux or Acadian Museum Home in the Longfellow Evangeline State Park is one of the most authentic and attractive in the state. The fram-

THE ACADIAN HOUSE MUSEUM

ST. MARTIN PARISH

ing by the 500-year-old moss-draped live-oak tree, only partially shown, accentuates the sturdiness of typical Creole construction. Though the customary outbuildings are gone, the original upper floors, beaded ceiling joists, doors, fenestration and trim are indicative of quality. The two upstairs bedrooms, with cradle, chamber pots, trundle bed, mosquito netting for the tester bed and the hand-woven bedding are genuine. The "stick" on the bed is used to smooth the feather-bed mattress.

21

Bedrooms

ACADIAN MUSEUM: *Punka*

The practical cloth on a scrolled wooden frame with its wooden sweep attached to a rope was swung back and forth by a young slave, ostensibly for cool air but more practically to keep the flies, which bedeviled both poor and rich man, from the food before the days of wire screens.

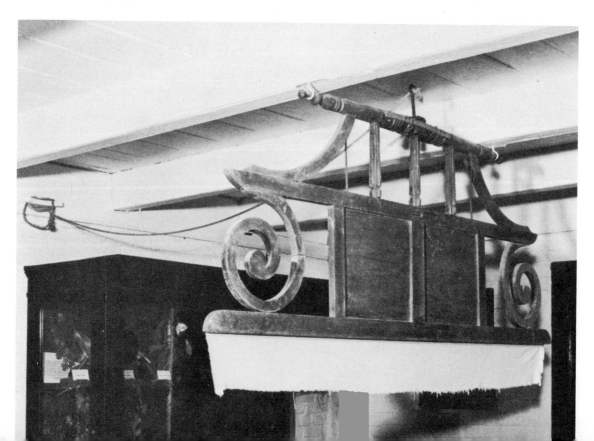

ACADIAN MUSEUM: *Mortar and Pestles*

Mortars and pestles spread with the use of Indian corn from Jamestown to the Pacific, to make hominy, to crack and grind where mill stone or stamping machinery was not available. This mortar was made from Louisiana's wood everlasting, a section of a young cypress tree perhaps 2000 years old. The pestles here were probably used daily to stamp out the day's supply of rice. A few can even now be found in use in the deep-delta and bayou sections.

On the side may be observed an ancient wool or thread reel sometimes called a weasel, for it had a clacker to mark a full turn, as in "Pop Goes the Weasel." The museum carefully preserves its seeds for the beautiful yellow cotton that slaves were allowed to grow in their free time. This they could not confuse with their master's crop.

ACADIAN MUSEUM: *Small House*

A typical reproduction of the small Cajun house with the stairway leading upward from the front porch and the outside shelf for washing dishes so that the minutiae of neighborhood behavior, friendly raillery and gossip could be passed along the bayou as quickly as if by telephone. During a stop for information at a village grocery and post office, word arrived that a bayou resident was to return from Korea. Driving along the road at as rapid a rate as possible for some five miles, the author could hear the news keeping pace.

AFTON VILLA: *Front Detail*

AFTON VILLA
WEST FELICIANA PARISH

Two houses in one: the older, built in the early 1820's, was completely incorporated, roof and all, into the present structure in 1849, by David Barrow for his second bride. Then perhaps the richest man in America, he could afford her whims. The remodeling took eight years. It evidently incorporated the changing ideas of Mrs. Barrow and the master builder. No information can be found concerning an architect. James Dakin, who was the architect for Louisiana's new capitol building that later so enraged Mark Twain's sense of propriety, perhaps stimulated Mrs. Barrow to follow the "latest style." The resulting forty rooms were in shocking contrast to other ante-bellum homes. The house was named after Barrow's daughter's favorite song, "Flow Gently, Sweet Afton."

AFTON VILLA: *Front Detail*

The illustration, a portion of the front façade with its Gothic peaks, points, arches and what in the Victorian period would have been called gimcrack, gives only a slight conception of the patterns followed for other façades where castellated turrets rise to great heights. There was nothing flimsy or light in the balconies, brackets, balusters and arches. They were solid, hand hewn and fashioned of Louisiana swamp cypress. Eclecticism was never more fanciful and persistent. As a result, contemporary architects recognize "pure" French Gothic, English Tudor, Greek Revival for a portion of the interior, and Moorish overtones. The main walls were of cypress covered with plaster, on the outside finished to simulate stone. Some interior rooms had stained glass, Moorish corridors. Other rooms were in carved cypress. There were rooms with exquisite plaster cornices and rosettes, some simulated Italian marble. The whole was filled with paintings, mirrors, objets d'art and furniture by Henry N. Siebrecht of Royal Street in New Orleans. There were fifteen bedrooms, many with small rooms attached where the personal body slave could sleep. The dining room, which seated forty persons, was supplied with food from a basement kitchen with a dumb waiter. This arrangement was unusual, for most planters preferred a separate kitchen for fire protection. A large acreage of woodland with generous plantings of flowers and shrubs, including the original "Afton Pink" azalea, and a continuation of a hundred-year-old yew maze added interest to the plantation.

26

AFTON VILLA: *Bedroom*

The master half-tester rosewood bed and the glass-fronted armoire are not the attraction of this room. In the corner may be seen one of the two weighty Carrara marble bathtubs known to have been in Louisiana plantation homes. This hollowed, shaped and decorated mass of marble would sit firmly on any floor stout enough to bear its weight. It had no drain, as there were no plumbing facilities when it was originally installed at Woodlawn plantation. The ornate screen at the end of the tub could be placed to assure privacy while bathing.

AFTON VILLA: *Front Hall and Stair*

Frasier Smith, in *White Pillars*, says this stairway and hall had carvings comparable to any English house of the period. The massive door was made of cypress from the plantation. The intricate hand carving was in marked contrast to the airy lightness of the circular stairway of the left rear hall.

AFTON VILLA: *Rear Stairway*

Gleaming white columns, surrounded by majestic magnolias and oaks, set the exterior pattern of magnificence for the fabled Southern planter. The crowning glory of the interior was a well placed, tastefully planned stairway. This generally rose from the main hallway, with a less ornate service stair relegated to the rear. Afton Villa, however, had a second "show" stairway which soared lightly and gracefully upward for three high stories.

28

ALEXANDER LOG CABIN

CLAIBORNE PARISH

On a low hill in Northwest Louisiana, George Washington Alexander built a double-pen log cabin. Carefully made of squared logs, with a raised floor, piers and chimneys of native field ironstone, this log home was a step in advance of the usual frontier log cabin with its dirt floor and roughly axed log walls. Erected in 1830, the house was dressed up at the turn of the century by the addition of siding and galleries front and back. The middle space between the original pens, the "dog trot," was enclosed and a door added. The attic was raised, and windows spaced in the gable ends to make a story-and-a-half dwelling. Today, with the one side serving as a hay barn and the other as a tenant house, the siding is disappearing to reveal the original construction.

Colonel John James Marshall bought a squatter's-right claim on which a sturdy log cabin had been built. It was near a clear-water spring in the rich hill lands of the northwestern part of the state, not far from the Texas line. He also bought surrounding sections of land, and brought slaves from his South Carolina home plantation in 1852. Using the original cabin as a corner, he added three additional pens or log rooms. The intervals which were customarily left open between each cabin were enclosed, thus giving an additional four large

ALLENDALE
DE SOTO PARISH

rooms. Two cabins have been removed and modern construction added. The three original rooms still retain their early charm. The open attic and enclosed chimney are unusual. Log-cabin attics were almost always enclosed for use.

ANGELINA: *Dovecote*

The Trosclair family, owners of several plantations, built Angelina in 1852. The two-and-one-half-storied house of brick and plaster was approached from the river by a long avenue of cedars. Some distance to the rear of the house there were a pair of dovecotes and a doll house or play house with its own fireplace, five feet in width. Each hexagonal picturesque dovecote, made of whitewashed brick, had its own weathervane, one a crowing cock, the

ANGELINA
ST. CHARLES PARISH

other a pacing horse with a flowing mane and tail. The Mississippi River has destroyed the main plantation buildings.

31

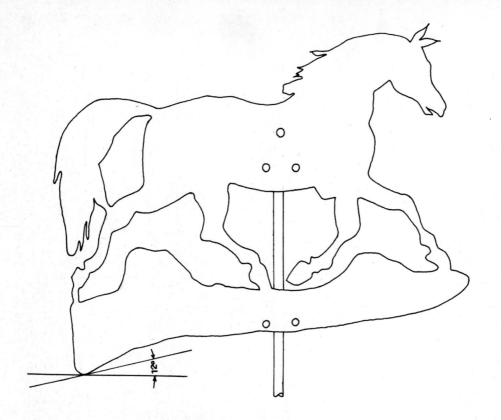

ANGELINA PLANTATION

The Weathervane   *Dollhouse*

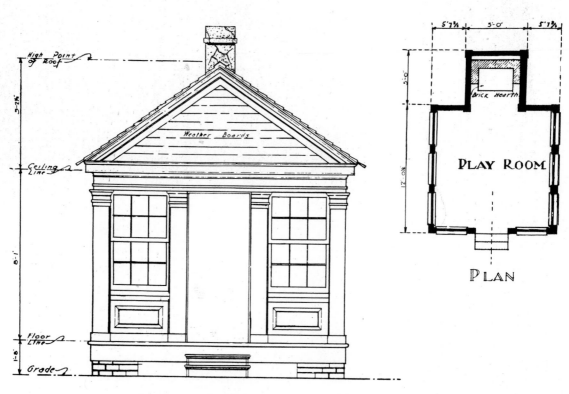

FRONT ELEVATION

ANGELINA: *Pigeonnier*

Built by a slave-owning free man of color in the eighteen-fifties, this southwestern Gulf Coast house betrays the absence of good architectural form. The center-pedimented portico is supported by four fluted columns, probably intended to be Corinthian. The second-floor gallery has wrought-iron railings. There are two small wings.

ARLINGTON
ST. MARTIN PARISH

ASHLAND: *Belle Helene*

Duncan Kenner was one of the wealthiest planters of the lush period before the Civil War. A descendant of two prominent American families living in Spanish colonial Louisiana, Kenner married into the incredibly rich Creole Bringier plantation family. In 1840 he commissioned James Gallier, Sr., to build a home for his bride, and named it after Henry Clay's Ashland. Kenner, active in state politics, was a United States Senator, a prominent member of the Confederate Congress and of the Confederate diplomatic service. Above all, he was a man who knew how to make money, and to spend it.

ASHLAND
ASCENSION PARISH

ASHLAND: *Belle Helene, partially restored*

Kenner spent a fortune on his Ashland racing stables. He gambled heavily and could afford to do so. Essentially he was a competent businessman who believed in political and economic order. His home and plantation grounds around it reflected this. Ashland was solidly and strongly built, as its appearance today attests even after long years of neglect and abuse. Differing from most other Louisiana plantation homes, Ashland's live-oak alleys were in the rear, planted in flat ovals leading to numerous accessory buildings, stables, offices, carriage houses, blacksmithies, storehouses, slave quarters, and finally to the sugar mills. Smaller shrubs and formal gardens beautified the approaches from the river.

Great square plastered brick columns rose flat from the ground, up and up, thirty feet to such a massive entablature that the low hipped roof could hardly be seen, even at a distance. Twenty-foot-wide galleries gave the same appearance from any side, although the wide hallway running "lengthwise" could be detected by its classical doorways. As was occasionally the practice in other Louisiana plantation homes, the stucco covering the brick walls was marked off in ashlar courses as if the buildings were of stone. The windows opened to the floor on both stories. The hall stairway of cypress with a mahogany railing was in keeping with the general theme of templelike sodidity.

Some of Louisiana's loveliest plantation homes were built in the hill sections of the state. Standing on a small bluff in East Feliciana, Asphodel is medium size, of Louisiana modified Greek Revival style. Two rooms wide, two deep, with no hall or "show" stairway to the second floor and with its high gables and dormers, the house is balanced by two small but tastefully set-back wings. The wings have classically pedimented porticoes. The front gallery has six plain Doric columns that are sprung from four-feet-high square

ASPHODEL
EAST FELICIANA PARISH

pedestals. Built in 1835 and given the classical poetic name for daffodil, Asphodel, the structure has changed little except for the enclosure of the rear gallery.

ASPHODEL: *Medallion*

Asphodel's two largest rooms faced the front gallery. One served as a library, the other as a formal drawing room; they were separated by wide sliding doors. Construction was of brick, plastered inside and out. The large octagonal ceiling ornamentation of stylized acanthus leaves in the drawing room lent interest to the otherwise plainly trimmed interior.

In the last decade of the eighteenth century Pierre Baillio erected this home, of raised mud and moss packed between cypress posts, on one of the several land grants he received from the Spanish government. His building site was near Bayou Rapides, which flowed into the Red River near Alexandria, where the falls in the river created a trading center. The cypress siding now on the structure may have been added when the wings were built several decades later.

PIERRE BAILLIO HOUSE
RAPIDES PARISH

PIERRE BAILLIO HOUSE: *Interior*

Wainscoted walls, paneled mantel and
a batten door with fine long old Spanish
wrought-iron hinges are in keeping with the
original post-and-mud construction. The wall-
papering is of course a modern refinement.

BARBARRA PLANTATION: *Garçonnière*

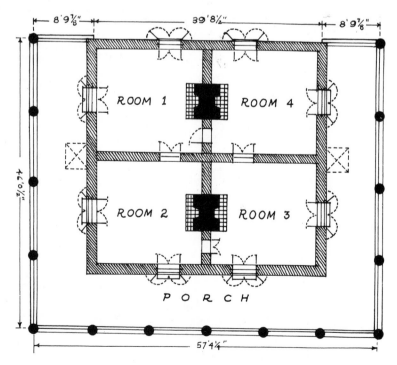

FLOOR PLAN

BARBARRA PLANTATION
ST. CHARLES PARISH

Unusually sturdily constructed and finished, this garçonnière is almost in the present city limits of New Orleans. Each room had handsome mantels and iron fireplaces. The nine-feet-wide galleries run at floor level for this two-room-deep and two-room-wide auxiliary plantation building. Each room is twenty feet square.

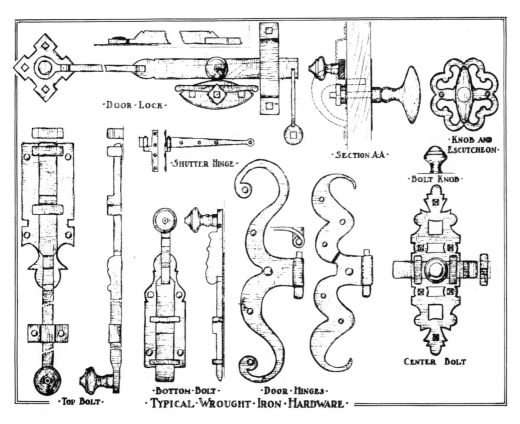

·DOOR·LOCK·

·SHUTTER·HINGE·

·SECTION·A·A·

·KNOB·AND·ESCUTCHEON·

·BOLT·KNOB·

·CENTER·BOLT·

·TOP·BOLT·

·BOTTOM·BOLT· ·DOOR·HINGES·
·TYPICAL·WROUGHT·IRON·HARDWARE·

Not far from Bayou Teche in the south-central section of the state, Francis D. Richardson, a friend of Edgar Allan Poe, built in 1850 a two-storied whitewashed brick home. Its six plastered round columns with bulbous bases rose to a light cornice. The second-floor gallery displays a wooden balustrade, making an attractive appearance. The roof is gabled, with chimneys at each end.

BAYSIDE
IBERIA PARISH

The first French colonial settlement in the Mississippi Valley was located at Natchitoches on Red River in 1714. The Red River later changed its course and the old channel became Cane River, along which there were clustered a number of plantation homes, of both white and colored slave owners. The Prudhommes were one of the most numerous of the plantation families. About 1830 they erected, of bousillage — a mixture of mud and moss between large timbers — an eighty-four-feet-long home for one of the family sons. In 1949, descendants Mr. and Mrs. Vernon Cloutier completely restored the dwelling, leaving only one of the interior room walls "uncov-

BEAUFORT
NATCHITOCHES PARISH

ered." The presence of huge underground cisterns and other suggestive evidence led at that time to the selection of the name Beaufort. Before the Civil War there was a room on the end of the front gallery, which later became known as the "stranger's" room because it provided overnight shelter to former Confederate soldiers making their weary way home.

A wealthy Belgian came to New Orleans in 1830. Acquiring some 7000 acres of rich land on Bayou Lafourche, he named his holdings and the new house he built to replace one burned by fire Belle Alliance. Although the family lived most of the time in New Orleans or Paris the new home was unusually large and pretentious, having twenty-six rooms. The large hallways had the square footage of many American homes. Decorative iron entrance gates led into a formal garden with classical statuary and fountains, but they are now things of the past. Screening on the upper gallery, the bane of architectural photography, diminishes the classic lines of the residence. The six square brick-and-plaster columns mount from low ground-level bases to the heavy, weighty entablature ornamented by dentils. A lighter contrast is attained by the extension of the front

BELLE ALLIANCE
ASSUMPTION PARISH

gallery to the sides, where graceful New Orleans-type colonnettes support a lower deck-type roof. The outside stair and porch railings are of cast iron. Another noteworthy feature is the ornamental iron plates over the bolts on the columns by which the gallery was hung. In most construction such bolts were concealed. Belle Alliance's interior is highly decorative and ornate.

The most prominent statesman of Louisiana's history, Judah P. Benjamin, erected Bellechasse in 1846. After leaving the United States Senate to serve in three cabinet posts of the Confederacy, he had to flee to England following the war. His home was moved twice to save it from the hungry maw of the Mississippi. Moving and neglect left their sordid marks on what was once an interesting deviation of style. The small third-story windows, like those one sees in old sections of New Orleans, opened to a gently pitched roof supported by tall square cypress columns rising from the ground level. The double verandas ran entirely around the house and had an outer stairway. The interior was originally well done, having a beautiful winding walnut stairway and highly ornamental plasterwork. The mansion has been demolished.

BELLECHASSE
PLAQUEMINES PARISH

45

The most pretentious house which the architect James Gallier, Jr., could conceive was commissioned by John Andrews in order to outbuild a neighboring planter, John Hampton Randolph, who had just completed Nottoway, a mere fifty-room mansion. Belle Grove had seventy-five rooms and an attic that was larger than many plantation homes. Both men were Virginians and had spent nearly twenty years of friendly but vigorous competition growing rich in Negroes, land, sugar and cotton, and times were booming. Both had numerous daughters and grandiose surroundings were needed to aid in obtaining the most suitable husbands. In terms of taste and beauty many plantation homes in the state surpassed both Belle Grove and Nottoway, but in massive

BELLE GROVE
IBERVILLE PARISH

bulk they were overpowering. They differed in style from all other country or town residences. Since they were completed in the decade before secession, the War and Reconstruction prevented the establishing of a trend.

Belle Grove had two high stories over a twelve-foot basement. The upper stories were of beautiful pink brick, plastered. There was no cohesion or conformity in its wings, except in color and massive bulk. Two overpowering sets of four Corinthian columns rose upward to an enlarged entablature of horizontal lines and large dentils, one of the most pleasing architectural executions of the plan. One set of columns was pedimented, the other not. Intricately carved capitals made from solid blocks of cypress were themselves six feet tall. The main portions of the building were tied together by the large entablature with its dentils, which were simulated on the rounded turrets. The wings had Roman arched window openings, while regular framed windows of various widths were used elsewhere. Some rooms had narrow balconies.

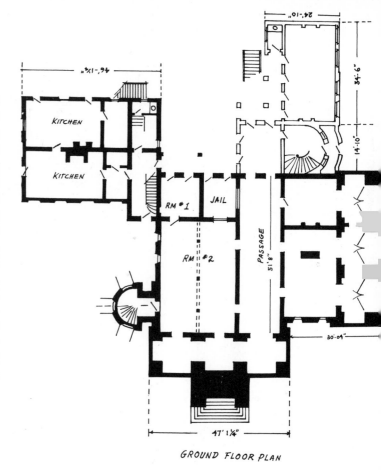

GROUND FLOOR PLAN

48

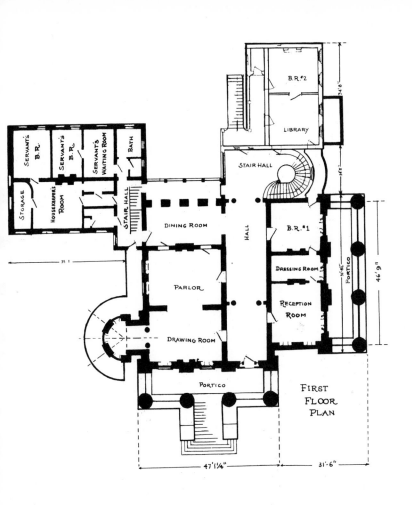

FIRST FLOOR PLAN

- STORAGE
- SERVANTS' B.R.
- SERVANTS' B.R.
- SERVANTS' WAITING ROOM
- BATH
- HOUSEKEEPER'S ROOM
- STAIR HALL
- DINING ROOM
- HALL
- B.R. #2
- LIBRARY
- STAIR HALL
- B.R. #1
- DRESSING ROOM
- RECEPTION ROOM
- PARLOR
- DRAWING ROOM
- PORTICO
- PORTICO

47'1¼" 31'-6" 46'9" 34'8" 14'2"

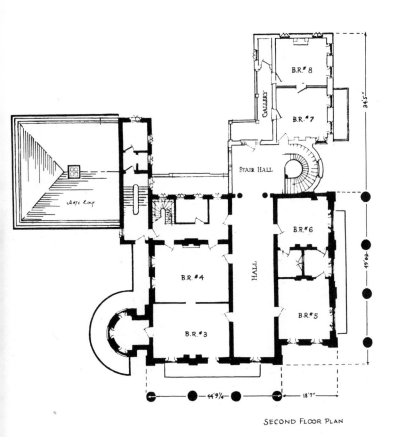

SECOND FLOOR PLAN

- SLATE ROOF
- B.R. #8
- GALLERY
- B.R. #7
- STAIR HALL
- B.R. #4
- HALL
- B.R. #6
- B.R. #3
- B.R. #5

34'5" 49'2" 14'9¾" 18'7"

DETAILS OF
CAST-IRON RAILING

Inside and out there was a profusion of pilasters and columns. Internal friezework and decorations were unstinted. Doorknobs and keyhole covers were in silver. Every aspect of building and furnishing was elaborate. The cash price was said to be $80,000, exclusive of furnishings, and with free labor and materials not being included. Translated into today's prices, such a figure would of course be enormous. Belle Grove was razed after World War II.

QUARTER ELEVATION · SCALE 3"= 1'-0"

HOOK FOR CHANDELIER

DETAILS OF PLASTER CENTERPIECE
DRAWING-ROOM AND PARLOR

BELLE GROVE: *Rear Ruins*

SIDE BALCONY
IRON WORK

DETAILS
OF
PILASTER & FRIEZE
AND
SECTIONS 'CL'

51

South of Natchitoches on Cane River, near the mulatto settlement of Isle Brevelle, Pierre Phanor Prudhomme built Bermuda in 1821. The plantation itself had been in the possession of the family since 1718. Other Prudhommes built homes along "La Côte Joyeuse" of Cane River. Of typically Louisiana Creole-styled construction, Bermuda has a raised basement with brick pillars and colonnettes supporting a high-pitched dormered roof. Here as well as in other Louisiana plantation homes, Negroes built well and enduringly for their masters. The interior, without a central hall, as rooms customarily were entered from the galleries, is plainly but neatly and carefully finished. A nicely made double door with a large glass fanlight separates the drawing room from the dining room. Bermuda is ac-

BERMUDA
NATCHITOCHES PARISH

credited with having grown the first cotton in the state. A slave blacksmith designed his own drilling tools and bored a water well. Bad luck occurred when oil was struck and the well had to be abandoned. Singularly, this plantation blacksmith's bits and drills anticipated those developed by modern oil drillers after years of trial and error.

BERMUDA: *Dining Room*

A large folding door with a tasteful fanlight opens one of the two front rooms, the parlor, into the dining room. Such room arrangement is typical of the better type of Creole construction. The fanlight was an extra touch of elegance, as was the punka.

This winged two-storied, plainly finished structure on the edge of the northeastern hills is just beyond the rich delta lands. The proportions of the main house are good. The six columns of no pure architectural order spring from high brick bases. They rise to a dentiled entablature that encircles the building and they enclose a balustraded front balcony. The tapered hip roof is matched by two small lower wings. The interior is very plainly finished, with a touch of refinement in the walnut stairway. The house had a cellar for storage.

BLAKEMORE
MOREHOUSE PARISH

A lazy loop of the Mississippi swinging near Lake Pontchartrain, where Bayou St. John almost connects the two, determined the location of New Orleans over a hundred miles upstream from the river's mouth. As Bayou St. John offered a short cut to the Gulf and easy access to New Orleans, a cluster of a half dozen plantation houses was built on the bayou. Among these was the Blanc house, now the property of a Catholic religious order to hold in trust to maintain its architectural purity. Built early in the nineteenth century, this

BLANC HOUSE
ORLEANS PARISH

somewhat pretentious home has heavier lower columns topped by light tapering colonettes. The doorways with fanlights and Corinthian columns add a distinctive touch.

55

Bocage — in English, Woody Retreat — was built as a wedding gift for Françoise Bringier Colomb in 1801. It was extensively remodeled in 1840. An oblong structure of brick below and wood above, its columns are interestingly arranged. Three large brick pillars are equally spaced on each end. Two smaller ones, close together, form the center. Bocage has an exceedingly high dentiled entablature that conceals the roof line and which makes the covered chimneys less conspicuous. The first-floor openings are plain; those of the up-

BOCAGE
ASCENSION PARISH

per are more ornate. At one time a stairway led upward from the lower gallery. The house was very nicely finished inside and, though neglected for periods of its history, it shines once again.

BONNER HOUSE
CLAIBORNE PARISH

It was a startling experience to drive along the iron-red roads of an isolated hill section of northwestern Louisiana and suddenly come upon the gaunt remains of what was, for these hill lands, an impressive ante-bellum home. Built in 1850, with the exception of an end chimney which was never completed, the home was originally approached by a circular half-mile landscaped drive. Two fluted columns rose from high brick pillars to a high portico whose roof continued back as a long narrow center gable. Three smaller columns supported the cornices of the balancing side wings. These rose from the gallery floors, as did the tall pilasters of the central portico. Wooden balustrades were used on the side galleries and on the gallery which once ran the full width on the rear. An unusual feature of the interior was a shallow entrance hall with an attractive stairway running down to the brick basement level, which contained a dining room, pantry, and kitchen. A plain door at one side of the hall opened to a simple stairway to the second story.

Located on the Red River in the center of the state is this raised Creole house. Its steep hipped roof incorporates the verandas which run across the front and halfway on each side. The house is raised for usage and protection from floods. The colonnettes are of plain squared cypress. The house itself is of cypress clapboards.

BROWNELL
GRANT PARISH

BRYAN LOG CABIN

BIENVILLE PARISH

The Bryan family left Georgia for Arkansas and after two years there, migrated to the hills of north-central Louisiana in the eighteen-thirties. Their new home had heart-pine sills fifty-seven feet long, resting on brick piers and, later, on piers cut from cypress trees several thousands of years old. Squared and pegged logs made two twenty-three-feet-square pens or rooms with an open narrow six-foot dogtrot. Contrary to usual custom the spaces between the logs were not chinked with mud, but the walls were battened with boards on the inside. The arrival of eleven children made necessary more space and lean-to rooms were added onto the back. An ample gallery was on the front.

BRYAN LOG CABIN: *Detail*

Wooden hinges on the rear half room doors were commonly used for barns, corn cribs and slave quarters in the northern part of the state, but seldom found except in very old log cabins. The Bryan dwelling also had hand-forged iron hardware. The homemade brooms by the door were the only kind used in this house in over a hundred years of occupancy.

59

BUENA VISTA

DE SOTO PARISH

BUENA VISTA: *Front Gallery (opposite)*

The wooden columns rising for only one of the two stories of this northwestern Louisiana home are mounted on brick piers which do not connect with the gallery floor. The balustrades, erected without the use of a single nail, are as strong and sturdy as when constructed in 1860. The entrance door opening into a wide hall curiously is not in the center of the building. The doorway, recessed and boxed, has fluted pilasters with side lights and a transom. The deep cornice is ornamented with dentils, as is the transom light below. The double hung windows run clear to the floor and are so tall one could use them as doors, walking through them with a hand raised above the head.

BUENA VISTA: *Drawing Rooms*

The size of the trim of the doorways with their sliding doors can be judged by the width of the chairs. The distance from the bay windows of one drawing room across the fourteen-foot hall to the bay windows of the opposite drawing room is sixty-five feet. The wide two-inch-thick floor boards of heart pine were grooved in a nearby sawmill and joined only after hot melted rosin was poured into each groove, as was the practice for each joint throughout the house. Care was taken to build this into a stout enduring home. The roof went untouched for nearly a hundred years, for the owner, Boykin Witherspoon, building just before the Civil War, saw that its three layers of shingles were boiled in linseed oil.

BUENA VISTA: *Mantel and Stairway*

So well proportioned is this plantation-finished mantel that it belies its size of ninety-six by forty-five inches. The baseboards and moldings on each are made from three-inch-thick planks.

From the rear of the wide hall the stairway climbs in broad easy sweeps to the attic floor. The sturdy shelf just before the third landing serves a double purpose, as a step to raise and lower the window, and as a shelf for hurricane-candle lights.

BUENO RETIRO: *René Beauregard*

In 1840 the New Orleans architect James Gallier, Sr., was said to have received a commission from the Marquis de Trava to build Bueno Retiro. This traditional-type house, like many others of the period, combined the one-room-deep raised basement and one story of Creole style with classical façades. The house, which has been "restored" by the National Park Service, is externally essentially the same, but liberties have been taken in raising the lower floor and adding partitions to make new rooms. Originally there were three rooms in the width, with a narrow side hall on the end for a plain stairway. Made of coarse or-

BUENO RETIRO
ST. BERNARD PARISH

ange plastered brick, the front and back had equally spaced massive columns rising to an adequate though not large entablature. The effect is one of charm. Bueno Retiro, with only six moderate-size rooms, seems larger. The low curved hip roof has two dormers on front and back and one on each end. The diamond wooden pattern of the veranda balustrades makes the difference in heights of the two floors less apparent.

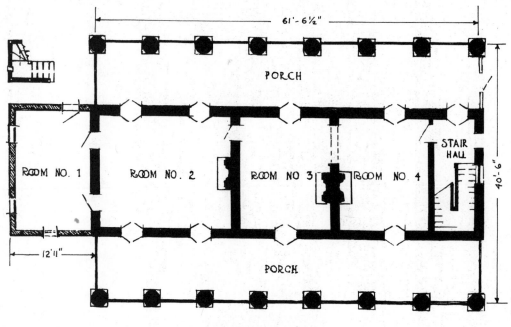

FIRST FL. PLAN

61'-6½"

40'-6"

12'11"

PORCH

ROOM NO. 1   ROOM NO. 2   ROOM NO. 3   ROOM NO. 4   STAIR HALL

PORCH

BUENO RETIRO: *Floor Plans*

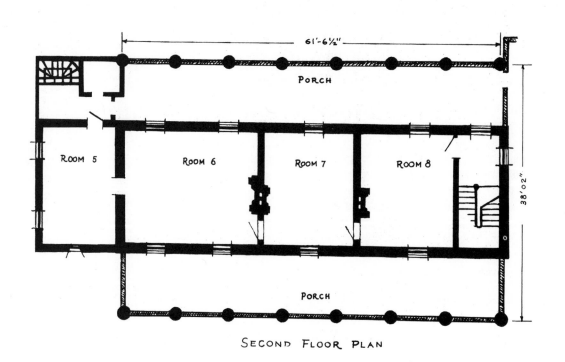

61'-6½"

38'02"

PORCH

ROOM 5   ROOM 6   ROOM 7   ROOM 8

PORCH

SECOND FLOOR PLAN

THE BURN

TENSAS PARISH

THE BURN: *Exterior*

In 1854 Zenith Preston built a story-and-a-half frame home with large rooms heavily plastered and frescoed. The hipped roof was supplied with two dormers on each elevation. The chimneys were built into the interior walls. The house was designed in an L shape. As the galleries ran on both sides of the L there were some 300 feet of gallery floors to be swept, a minor problem with slave labor, but a major one for a housekeeper today. In the rich Mississippi delta lands in the northern part of the state there was a sufficiency of wealth available to build substantially.

THE BURN: *Interior*

The handsome marble mantel is indicative of the quality of The Burn's interior construction. The door hardware in the main rooms is silver plated.

65

CAT-AND-DAUB CHIMNEY
NATCHITOCHES PARISH

CAT-AND-DAUB CHIMNEY: *Detail*

In only a few northern sections of Louisiana were stones available to build chimneys or provide foundations. Money and skill could convert the right kind of clay into fireproof brick. Many small plantation owners in the early periods built their slave-cabin chimneys by the use of short cross sticks thickly plastered with mud. Such a primitive chimney had to be rebuilt regularly for safety's sake. Loss of mud from inside heat or outside rain meant disaster. This North Louisiana Cane River chimney was newly repaired.

CAVETT
BOSSIER PARISH
CAVETT: *Two-Story Log Cabin*

The author knows of only two extant two-story Louisiana log cabins. Both are in the northwestern section of the state. Both have long since been sided over with milled lumber. The Cavett home was built in 1848 about the same time as was the Plant-Montgomery Log Cabin.

Cedar Grove is said to have been built at the end of the French Colonial era or the beginning of the Spanish. The exterior appears to be of the period 1840-1850. The gabled house has nine square brick columns with narrow caps that support an upper gallery complete with square colonnettes and a nicely turned balustrade.

CEDAR GROVE
RAPIDES PARISH

Each visitor to Chretien Point, whether professional architect, lover of fine homes or mere casual passerby, senses that here is a special atmosphere savoring of old Creole Louisiana. While in need of paint, plaster and shutter replacements, the house still appears from the outside very much as it must have to its builder, Hypolyte Chretien. Of course the roof was then of shingles rather than galvanized tin. The interior certainly would sadden the original owner, for today the softness of the pasteled rooms richly furnished is gone. Plaster has fallen and mud daubers have invaded the unused second story.

CHRETIEN POINT
ST. LANDRY PARISH

Chretien Point is sixty-three feet wide by forty-seven feet deep, each story being twelve feet in the clear. Each of the three front rooms of both floors has its own entrance door. To the rear there are matching half rooms, one of which contains the stair with a walnut rail. The building contract is registered at the parish court house in nearby Opelousas.

The contractors agreed to build for $7000, an illusory figure, for Chretien was also to furnish all the wood necessary, including timbers, planks, shingles, laths, and the brick and lime for plastering. This was not all, for there was the housing of the contractors and their workmen, plus the hauling of materials, and the service of as many of Chretien's slaves as was required during the four-year building period, 1831-1835.

Chretien Point is rich in history and romance. Rumor has it that the plantation served as a favorite way station for smugglers. Lying on the edge of the Louisiana prairie, it was a participating part of the rough frontier, as the widowed owner discovered when she was forced to shoot off the head of one of a gang of five thieves. The residence itself was spared from burning when a Union general returned the Masonic sign waved by the enfeebled owner from the upper gallery. All the other outbuildings, the cotton, forage and cattle were destroyed.

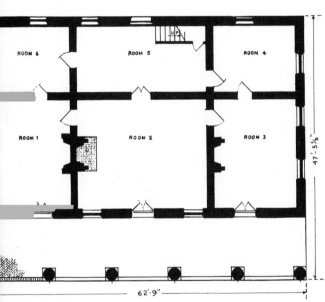

FIRST FLOOR PLAN

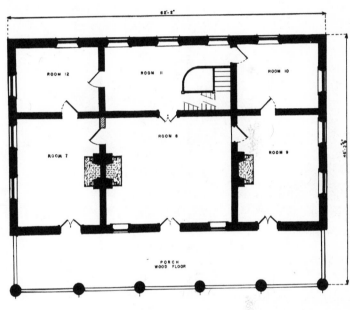

SECOND FLOOR PLAN

CHRETIEN POINT: *Upper Gallery*

Deeply recessed doors indicate the "four brick thickness" of the outside wall construction. Cypress paneled wainscoting runs beneath the double hung windows with their circular headings. These once had the half-circle side venetian shutter blinds which can be seen on the lower floor. The richness of door and window details, the fanlight transom and headers are indications of how well the Georgian mode could be blended with Louisiana Creole Greek Revival architecture.

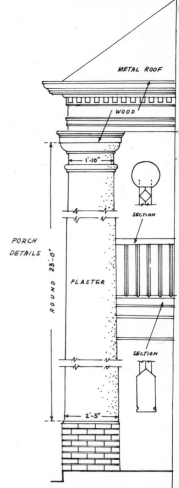

PORCH
DETAILS

METAL ROOF

WOOD

ROUND 25'-0"

PLASTER

1'-10"

2'-3"

SECTION

SECTION

CHRETIEN POINT: *Façade Detail*

The staunch Tuscan columns sitting on their low square bases are of plastered brick. They support a gallery with a plain wooden balustrade, and a modest entablature with "dentil and Modillion blocks." Concealed in the cornices are the still functioning cypress gutters, as large as half a tree. The original plans provided for stairs to ascend from the lower brick gallery floor to the gallery above. There is no evidence that this was done. While the present illustration shows the upper portion of the lower first floor to be painted, originally only the upper-gallery wall was plastered white.

CHRETIEN POINT: *Detail, First-Floor Stairway*

A simple but charming "home planned" stair and railing at the rear of the home.

70

CHRETIEN POINT: *Salon*

The building contract called for plank ceiling and two-coat plastered and papered walls except in the "large room," illustrated here, which was to have three whitened plaster coats for ceilings and walls, with "hard finished cornice all around." There was also an ornate ceiling medallion. The dress mantel is of verde-antique Italian marble. The Ionic columns with black onyx caps support a black onyx curved shelf. The front panel of the mantel is chastely carved. The glass door and door-frame trim is similar in pattern to that used in few other houses of the period.

Salon Mantel

THE COTTAGE (ST. FRANCISVILLE):
Rear

After the beginning of this home in 1811
additions were made so that by the time of
the Civil War it was the L-shaped residence
shown here. The two-story dormered center
building flanked by a single gabled extension
is photographed from the rear. Built low on the
ground, the earlier portion has smaller colonnettes than the wing. The Cottage fortunately
has retained many of the original attached

THE COTTAGE
(ST. FRANCISVILLE)
WEST FELICIANA PARISH

buildings, including the plantation school, milk
house, kitchen and slave quarters. Note the
moss and fern growing upon the live-oak limb
in the foreground.

CREOLE HOUSE: *Wall Detail*

CREOLE HOUSE
WINN PARISH

When the author and his wife approached this Natchitoches Parish house one August morning the "grandfather" was killing a chicken. Several hours later while we were photographing rafter construction in the attic, the other members of the family returned from picking cotton. The most tantalizing odors drifted up, frying chicken, okra, tomatoes and onions cooking together, and corn bread baking in the oven. The house, of French Creole origin, though now a Negro tenant house, is typical of early construction methods. Note the mud and moss packed into spaces between cypress posts. The upper left corner illustrates inner construction. Such materials were not a poor man's substitute. The house was carefully built; even the ceiling plate of this outside wall is double-grooved as a finishing touch.

Near the coast in southwestern Louisiana stands a raised rural French colonial home with a steep hipped roof covering the rear and front galleries. All is very plainly but enduringly done. Obviously many changes and repairs have been made over the years, such as wooden siding, non-matching rear and front gallery piers, the enclosure of the rear gallery and new fenestration and blinds. It is reputed to have much of the original 1765 furniture.

DARBY (BALDWIN)
ST. MARTIN PARISH

DARBY (NEW IBERIA)
IBERIA PARISH

Darby was probably built in the decade before the battle of New Orleans, and its architectural style is Louisiana Creole untouched by the refinements of Georgian fenestration. Though not large, it is an interesting house with a pathetic history. A sister and two brothers, educated in Paris, moving in the élite circles of the state, were impoverished by the Civil War. They retired to Darby, eking out a bare living. When one brother "lowered himself" by selling milk to the townspeople of New Iberia, in his frock coat, the other brother lived out his life in his half of the house without conversation. At times they would "sing" warnings about cows and chickens and family troubles to each other. Naturally the house was in bad repair when it passed into the possession of other heirs a generation ago. The lower floor of brick has a central hallway from front to back. In the rear of this hall a small plain stairway leads up to the matching hallway of the main floor. Here the rooms have higher ceilings with plain carefully executed paneling and trim. The top of a brick underground cistern, still in use, can be seen in the right foreground.

DARBY (NEW IBERIA): *Columns and Stairs*

These columns show their age: all the plaster is gone, the mortar is going and the soft rounded bricks made on the plantation are about ready to dissolve back into the soil. The colonnettes and the balustrades are still upright on the front side, but Darby seems doomed. The stairway placed at the end of the gallery, though clumsily rebuilt, is characteristic of this type of house. Even here close examination will show that the timbers were painstakingly beaded both on the stairs and exposed rafters.

Built in 1787-1790 Destrehan, a few miles up the river from New Orleans, was one of the great plantation homes constructed under the Spanish flag. The building contract, discovered by one of Louisiana's leading restoration architects and professor of Architecture at Tulane University, Samuel Wilson, notes that a free man of color, as a carpenter, woodworker and mason, signed a contract to build this home, thirty-five feet deep and sixty feet in length. The original owner·died and the property was purchased by Jean d'Estrehan de Beaupre in 1802 as a home for his wife and fourteen children. The year of 1787 was too early for the Greek Revival influence of great white columns and other refinements now in the house. Indications are that considerable changes were made before the Civil War. Early in the present century an oil company converted the residence into a clubhouse. For

DESTREHAN
ST. CHARLES PARISH

many years it was well maintained. Unfortunately wire screening and untrimmed shrubbery have lessened its attractiveness.

Symmetrical wings added in 1810 are of the same basic West Indian raised basement style. The deep verandas are supported by heavy plain Doric columns. The wide sweeping lines of the roof are of particular interest, as is the unusual smallness of the dormers of each main façade. There are wide well-proportioned side-lighted doors, front and back. The moldings and window and door trim are in keeping.

77

Eugene DuChamp, a refugee from the French West Indies, built this plantation home, in the heart of the Acadian country, on a ridge near St. Martinville, about the year 1855. Cautiously he incorporated a raised brick basement for his wooden story-and-a-half gabled and dormered house. Eight square brick columns support the balustraded veranda. Smaller turned wooden colonnettes rise to the roof line.

DU CHAMP
ST. MARTIN PARISH

Said to be modeled after Andrew Jackson's Hermitage, Ducros has eight square tall columns supporting wide galleries. The low hipped roof has a wide shaped entablature in good taste. The central doors on each floor are side-lighted and heavily transomed. Made of wood, this sugar-cane plantation residence was completed just as the Civil War began. Named for the original Spanish land grant near the Gulf in the south-central section of the state, the site has an altitude of ten feet. The setting enhances its charm.

DUCROS
TERREBONNE PARISH

ELDORADO
POINTE COUPEE PARISH

The fabulously rich David Barrow of Afton Villa presented to his son Bart (Bartholomew II) as a wedding gift a large plantation, complete with a new wooden plantation home. A somewhat modest dwelling with six square wooden columns and large dormers, it had in the immediate rear a pair of two-storied brick garçonniéres. When the house was built in 1857 a complete hand-painted set of china, said to have cost $1500, handsome silverware and a Mallard rosewood bedroom set were included. Afton Villa workmen duplicated the quality interior plaster work. An elegant small stair added dignity for the very rich owner of 226 slaves living in forty-seven cabins, producing 624,000 pounds of sugar and 52,000 gallons of molasses as staple crops, in addition to foodstuffs for the plantation livestock and slaves.

There are few if any Greek Revival homes in Louisiana which rival the classic beauty of this four-square ante-bellum mansion. It is located north of St. Francisville in the northeastern corner of the state. Built in 1828-1832 by one of the remarried daughters of the Barrow plantation dynasty, she had considerable difficulty in locating a competent "architect-contractor." She sought for such in Ohio, Maryland and other states before employing James Hammon Coulter.

Contemporary plan books provided designs for exterior and interior trim and woodwork. These were executed from plantation lumber shipped to the steam mills of Cincinnati, Ohio. The house walls are of lath and plaster. Ellerslie has eight great Doric columns on each façade. These ascend from sturdy cypress sills resting on brick piers to an entablature five feet high. The present owner, Mr. Edward Percy, in replacing a portion of

ELLERSLIE
WEST FELICIANA PARISH

the five-foot architrave in the right-hand corner could not find such massive wide lumber and had to resort to substitute materials. The entablature with its two horizontal lines of wooden trim running around the four façades, is Ellerslie's major deviation from Greek Revival form. Originally a large glass-enclosed belvedere surmounted the hipped roof. Both galleries originally had a simple balustrade blending well with the square templelike general appearance. Each window opens on a gallery and has a divided split paneling below which swings open so that each window be-

comes a door. It is said that the builders purposely tilted one side of the swinging panels to provide a crack for a flow of air to make the chimney draw well. Black-marble mantels and elaborate ceiling-plaster rosettes decorate the twenty-two-foot square lower rooms. A wide central hall with a beautiful circling stair adds spaciousness.

ELLERSLIE: *Stair*

At the end of the wide hall running through the center of Ellerslie is an entrancing curving stairway turning upward to the plastered attic storerooms above the second floor.

Almost lost in the rich sugar and sweet-potato bayou lands near the south-central Gulf Coast is this attractive plantation home built in the late 1850's. Neither pretentious nor lavish, this wooden two-storied home is typical of its period. Its windows and square columns are well proportioned. In the rear is a commodious slave-built wash house.

ENTERPRISE
ST. MARTIN PARISH

Slave Jail

EVAN HALL
ASSUMPTION PARISH

The original "Big House" built on an old Spanish land grant is gone, but the slave quarters are in good repair. Facing each other across the customary wide plaza, the brick buildings are of single- and double-family size. The unbalanced long gabled roof provides needed shade from the lower South's intense heat. The "jail" lacks this comfort. The plantation has long been known as the McCall plantation.

Double Slave Cabin

Evergreen has an individuality that sets it apart from other Louisiana plantation establishments. The pigeonniers, offices and some of the outbuildings are thought to be of much earlier construction than the central house, which was erected in the eighteen-twenties. The portico was probably added soon after to provide a staging for a single circling free-standing stair, recently doubled, which is a distinguishing feature of modern Evergreen. Eight Doric columns are spaced across the front, with two additional for the portico. As in other early houses, two side galleries run part way down each side. They are one column deep. Dormers extend from the sides of the modest hipped roof, which is surmounted by a plain balustrade. Evergreen was planned as an estate running back from the Mississippi River above New Orleans. There were two

EVERGREEN
ST. JOHN THE BAPTIST PARISH

widely separated alleys of three rows of trees; the outer of live oaks, the next of magnolias and the inner of shorter growing cedars. A formal garden of shrubs and smaller annuals and perennials amid shelled paths led to the house. Each side was carefully balanced with pigeonniers, garçonnières, offices, cook's house, carriage houses and outbuildings leading back to the slave quarters, the sugar mills and other plantation buildings. Fantastically, the privies and stables were done in pure Greek Revival style.

From Shreveport in northwest Louisiana, an oxcart highway ran from the head of Red River navigation westward to Mexico. On this highway, not far from the border of the sovereign Republic of Texas, a six-room log house was built in 1842. Now neatly sided, with the addition of a small portico and shutters, it has the appearance of a modern home.

FLOURNOY-WISE LOG CABIN
CADDO PARISH

FOREST HOME
DE SOTO PARISH

A double log cabin was built here in the 1830's, in the extreme western part of northern Louisiana, adjacent to the new Republic of Texas. Captain James Foster built the present home just at the outbreak of the Civil War. The house passed into the hands of the Fulli-love family and then to the Johns family. It was never fully finished. M. Robbins was the master builder. The house once had a half-basement dining room and kitchen, and still retains an enclosed stair to the attic.

Bedroom

FOREST HOME: *Parlor*

The second Agricole Fuselier de la Claire was the descendant and relative of numerous French and Spanish Creole families who settled along the bayous of the extreme southern part of what was, at the time of the building of Fuselier, the territory of Orleans. Fuselier was Creole in style. It was small, one and a half rooms deep, with a raised basement of brick with stucco and wood above. The hip roof was steep and dormered. Six low, well proportioned brick columns rose to the gallery. Eight smaller wooden colonnettes continued to the roof line.

Interestingly Fuselier as illustrated is now considerably changed. In 1961 the chimneys, the stairs and the raised brick basement were torn away, the upper story was then loaded on a barge and towed along Bayou Teche from Baldwin to Jeanerette. The upper story made

FUSELIER
IBERIA PARISH

of Creole bousillage (mud and moss between cypress timbers) made the trip without, as the new owner declared, the loss of a pound of mud. Incidentally this mud has been hardening for 150 years. At the new location concrete culverts, well plastered, made new columns for the remodeled basement which was converted to formal living quarters. The floor joists and flooring of the upper story became the new ceiling, with exposed ceiling joists for the lower floor.

Reputed to have been built shortly after the Louisiana Purchase, this south Louisiana raised-basement plastered brick house has always had excellent care. Its stairway mounts from the lower gallery. The lower floor and the gallery were paved with extra large imported octagonal tiles. The heavy hipped roof gives the feeling of squatness along its 100-foot front. Only one of the original two pigeonniers which flanked the rear sides remains standing. At each front corner there were originally two large underground cisterns. These have been filled in, one serving as a child's bathing pool, the other for a flower planting.

GLENDALE
ST. JOHN THE BAPTIST PARISH

GLENDALE: *Interior (opposite page)*

Glendale's interiors were ornamented by paneling, wainscoting, and cornices of wood. All these were incorporated in the setting for the fireplace with its pilasters which rise to form a double cap on the molding. The house, one and a half rooms deep with a back gallery, has to the left of this fireplace a glassed window into the half-sized room to the rear.

In the extreme northeast corner of Louisiana near the Arkansas line, the rich Mississippi River delta lands provided cotton wealth in abundance. Of the plantation mansions which this wealth produced, the Vicksburg campaign, fire and flood have left but a few. One of these, Gossypia, built in 1856, in exterior at least, is more akin in spirit to Mediterranean waters than those of Louisiana. No columns, not even colonnettes, no raised basement, no extensive verandas, no adequate provision for cooling breezes, make it a house apart, in its day more so than to a modern viewer. The small second floor, finished as the lower with a thick plaster coating, has windows that are mere slots. Local legend absurdly has Confederate soldiers jumping through these to their death when trapped by Union soldiers. Gossypia, meaning cotton, has a short wide hall with an attractive two-stage stairway.

GOSSYPIA
EAST CARROLL PARISH

GOSSYPIA: *Interior*

Plasterwork friezes, either molded or handworked, as in this case, were the result of a desire to obtain the ultimate in elegance for a drawing room. Modern lighting fixtures unfortunately often mar the effects of center rosettes.

92

Beauty is a rare and fleeting sensory experience to be seized at a propitious moment. But beauty is also to be contemplated and re-experienced. Greenwood's four classical temple façades offer many changing facets during varied seasons to the eye, and to the eye of the mind. In 1830 William Ruffin Barrow conceived the effect made possible in this illustration by digging clay for his brick adjacent to the house to make a reflection pool. Oliver Pollock, a friend of the Spanish governors, was the original owner of the plantation grant, which he sold to help finance aid and munitions for George Rogers Clark's expedition against Kaskaskia and Vincennes during the Revolutionary War.

The Barrow family were perhaps the most prolific builders of substantial plantation homes

GREENWOOD
WEST FELICIANA PARISH

in Louisiana. They seemed to have an aversion for brick construction. Greenwood is therefore of lath and plaster, with only the columns of brick and plaster. These twenty-eight Doric shafts, reaching upward over thirty feet, are unusual in that they do not spring from the ground or piers, but from a raised stylobate. Unlike most of the state's large homes of the period, there is no second-story veranda. The entablature is also individual in its decorative design of triglyphs. The windows are plain with no Georgian influences.

GREENWOOD: *Mantel*

The 100-foot square of Greenwood is divided by a seventy-foot-long central hall with the customary four rooms on each floor. Also as was usual in luxurious homes of the period, silver plate was used for the huge locks and door hinges. Gold window cornices and imported mantels were in accord with the taste and financial means of the wealthy owners. The mantel of white and black marble speaks of its own oneness with the charm of Greenwood.

Although this home was located in the vicinity of the many-columned Greek temple "Greenwood," they were different. This floor plan and elevation shows the one-story brick combination kitchen, smokehouse, dairy and well. The building was gabled with a parapet front and back. It measured thirty feet by twenty-seven feet, plus a seven-foot porch.

GREENWOOD (VENTRESS)
WEST FELICIANA PARISH

NORTH·EAST ELEVATION

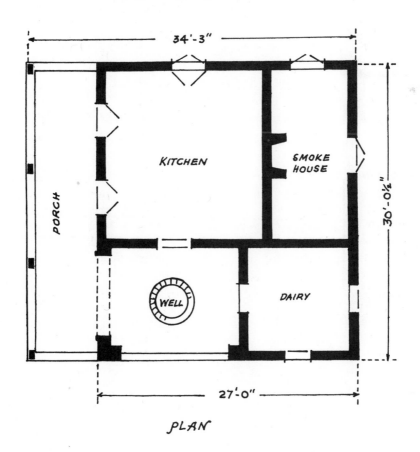

PLAN

HATCH HOUSE
RICHLAND PARISH

HERMITAGE
ASCENSION PARISH (opposite page)

This Boeuf River home in northeast Louisiana, an unpretentious, pleasant story-and-a-half plantation house of the early eighteen-fifties, seems in perfect accord with the rich cotton lands of the region. It was built of milled lumber with a porch on the front and a wooden patterned balustrade.

Marius Pons Bringier purchased a plantation and house facing the Mississippi about halfway between New Orleans and Baton Rouge. In 1812 he remodeled the brick-between-post building and gave it to his son, returning from Paris, as a wedding gift. A patriotic new American admirer of Andrew Jackson, he named the newly remodeled home the Hermitage. A few decades later, as sugar provided ever increasing wealth, certain changes were made. The Louisiana Creole second-story gallery sitting on top of brick columns was attached to the new columns, which reached an extended and enlarged entablature. Wood, not iron, was used for a simple balustrading. The floor plan, of a central hall and two rooms on each side, was probably changed to permit a stairway in the hall, though still retaining a stair on the inside

of the back gallery. Also added was a large
seventy-foot brick ballroom with two black-
marble mantels to add elegance. The house
seems to sit low. Marred by its present-day tin
roof and lack of paint, it stolidly faces the
hungry Mississippi which year by year and
acre by acre inches its way toward its doors.

HERMITAGE: *Columns*

The original portion of the Hermitage
was built of *briquette entre poteaux* and the
columns were added at the peak of the owner's
wealth. The Doric simplicity of line, eight
columns in front and six to the side, is in complete harmony with the building they enclose,
the palmettos at their feet, the live oaks that
guard them, the mighty levee which confronts
them and the rich wet soil which made them
possible. The iron plate of the corner column,
once concealed by plaster, is a tie to the floor
joists of the gallery.

William Barrow Floyd in his recent *The Barrow Family of Old Louisiana* documents the genealogy and history of a prolific plantation family, the wealthiest in the state. Their first home was Highland, built in 1805 in the West Florida Parishes of Spanish Florida. Later, under United States sovereignty, they became the East Florida Parishes of Louisiana. Located halfway between Natchez, Mississippi, and Baton Rouge, the house still stands. Although altered and enlarged from time to time, Highland never became a Louisiana type. Mr. Floyd believes it was modeled after a drawing from Asher Benjamin's *The Country Builder's Assistant* of 1797, of the Federal style so popular in the Carolinas and Tennessee.

HIGHLAND
WEST FELICIANA PARISH

Built of cypress clapboards, only the shutters were milled in Cincinnati, from cypress sent from the plantation. As was customary at this early date, bar iron was purchased to make the few necessary nails and hardware. Poplar wood was used in the doorway and entrance hall and in the wainscoting. The house boasted a Palladian window on the second floor. Eventually there were thirty-seven slave cabins at Highland, housing some four to five times as many slaves.

98

The site of the Houmas-Burnside house was owned by the Houmas Indians. It passed through the hands of Daniel Clark, the Marquis de Auconne, the Bringiers and the Wade Hampton and Preston families to those of an Irish immigrant, John Burnside, and on and on to its present owners. The Bringiers built the original dwelling, here hidden but connected on the second-floor level in the rear. In 1840, four decades or more later, the present main structure was completed. Later occupants added balustrades and gimcrack, but now once again the house shines in its pristine glory. Its immense modified Doric columns stand among the whitest in the state, six across the front, supporting galleries with their wooden balus-

HOUMAS-BURNSIDE

ASCENSION PARISH

trades. Only the belvedere, with its straight-lined windows in contrast to the curves of the dormer windows, lends a clashing note. The house is flanked by pigeonniers and garçonnières.

HOUMAS-BURNSIDE: *Garçonnière*

For maturing boys and their guests the garçonnières gave privacy and added space. Small or large, with living quarters in this instance on the second story, they as a rule flanked the larger Creole plantation homes. Here the hexagonal garçonnière, dwarfed by immense trees, seems to offer a peaceful haven for quiet meditation.

100

HURST
ORLEANS PARISH

This plantation home, now surrounded by metropolitan New Orleans, was dismantled under careful architectural supervision and moved a few miles to the Bayou St. John area. Built in 1836, its raised basement originally included a slave jail. The walls are of brick with enclosed chimneys. The gabled ends are wooden. Classic lines were incorporated by the use of fluted columns with plain caps, and a Doric entablature with triglyphs. The central entrance changes to Ionic columns with a recessed oddly paneled door. The door knob is set very low. The side lights are set above paneling which is widely used, as is wainscoting for the interior of the house. Hurst's high baseboards, wainscoting, paneling, arched framing of doors, intricate variations of winding-vine carvings, circles and flutings give combinations not found elsewhere in the state. Veranda windows have split panels on hinges to swing open.

Above New Orleans, just a few years before the Louisiana Purchase, the prominent
Fortier family built this Creole dwelling of
goodly size. Two rooms deep was the basic
plan. Each room on each floor had one or more
entrances on the galleries. There were no halls
and only one sneak stairway for the use of the
personal servants. Contrary to usual practice,
the rooms varied in size and proportions. The
house is younger than Parlange but has the
same plainness to the point of severity. There

KELLER HOMEPLACE
ST. CHARLES PARISH

are simple light cornices and balustrades.
Turned wooden colonnettes are supported by
brick-and-plaster pillars with unfinished capi-

tals and bases. These reminded the architect J. Fraser Smith of Parlange. The stairways leading from the lower gallery were originally on the right-front and left-rear corners and are quite different from those at Parlange, although the latter evinces unknown changes, particularly in the rear elevation. The basement floors were of brick, or of alternating blue and white marble. Keller Homeplace used more individualistic and extensive grillwork in lieu of walls and windows than is known to have been used in any other plantation house. Since the basement contained a wine room whose racks held several thousand bottles of wine the grills needed to be carefully placed. The upper level was floored with two-inch-thick cypress. The walls were heavily plastered and those of the upper level papered with imported French blocked paper which still remains. The plantation had the customary outbuildings including the kitchen, dairy, carriage house, pigeonniers, stables, and others.

KELLER HOMEPLACE: *Grill Work*

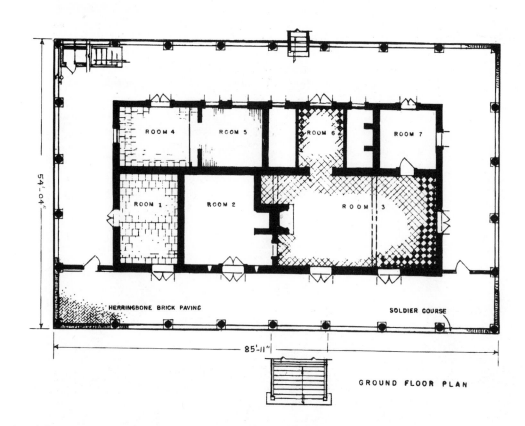

ROOM 4 ROOM 5 ROOM 6 ROOM 7

ROOM 1 ROOM 2 ROOM 3

54'-04"

HERRINGBONE BRICK PAVING SOLDIER COURSE

85'-11"

GROUND FLOOR PLAN

KELLER HOMEPLACE

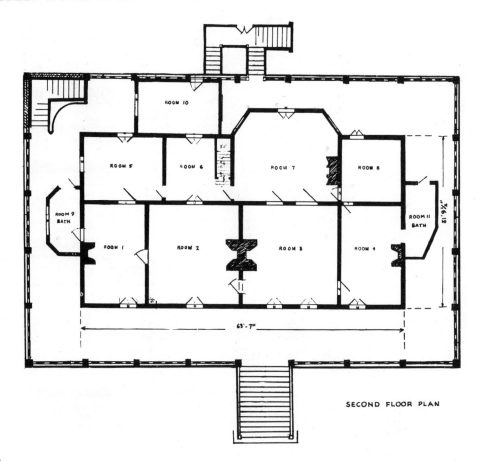

ROOM 10

ROOM 5 ROOM 6 ROOM 7 ROOM 8

ROOM 9
BATH

ROOM 11
BATH

ROOM 1 ROOM 2 ROOM 3 ROOM 4

51'-9½"

63'-7"

SECOND FLOOR PLAN

104

Basement Window

Mantel

KELLER HOMEPLACE

Old Cypress Shingles

Lying south and east of New Orleans, the vast acres of Pierre Antoine Bienvenu, who arrived from Canada in 1725, became a part of the battleground against the British in 1815. Here in 1759 he is said to have built a portion of the home which his English-educated granddaughter was later to name Kenilworth. Changes were made in the early nineteenth century when the original one story was enlarged and a story and half added. The brick plastered lower walls change to cypress above. The somewhat peaked hipped roof breaks for the seldom used double-windowed dormers. The window sashes are of later origin. The columns of the lower story are squarely made

KENILWORTH
ST. BERNARD PARISH

at the bottom and taper as they rise. The upper colonnettes are square to the top of the wooden balustrade and then round until they meet the roof. A stairway rises from the side veranda to the second veranda. The interior trim is somewhat bulky: the plantation labor employed was not too skilled.

LADY OF THE LAKE
ST. MARTIN PARISH

Despanet de Blanc received a Spanish land grant of 3200 acres in the watery plains region of what is today central-southwestern Louisiana. He built his home during the American Revolution in a rolling ridge, calling it La Couteau. Using an oversize brick for the raised basement, which had an imported tile floor, and an upper story of *briquette entre poteaux*, he thickly plastered the upper walls. These he later sided with wood. His large fireplaces were fitted with cast-iron grates and marble mantels. Short pillars supported the gallery which surrounded the house. Above these were slim colonnettes to the roof line. The stairway shown is not original, though a sneak interior stairway is still in place.

LAKEWOOD: *Medallion*

A. C. Watson built Lakewood in 1854 in
Tensas Parish, on the banks of a beautiful oxbow lake that was once the channel of the
Mississippi. At the outbreak of sectional hos-
tilities he withdrew $80,000 in gold. Sixty
thousand he used to form an artillery company, twenty thousand he buried. After the
war $15,000 was recovered. The family sought
the remainder, in vain, for eighty years. Then
someone cultivating a rosebed uncovered a
china teapot containing $5000 in gold, just in
time to save the plantation from foreclosure
during the depression. One-storied Lakewood
was built of cypress, lathed and plastered inside. This medallion in the right-front room

LAKEWOOD
TENSAS PARISH

is of iron and brightly painted. The indistinct
center of the illustration is a light bulb hanging from a five-foot cord. The owner of the
residence was decorating at the time this picture was taken and remarked, "Plastered walls
simply will not endure in Louisiana!" This
room, after a hundred years, had only a single
small crack in its plaster.

LAND'S END
DE SOTO PARISH

Stylized acanthus leaves were commonly used for plaster designs during the ante-bellum period. This hall medallion differs in that the leaves were made of papier-mâché.

Colonel Henry Marshall, active in the nullification controversy in South Carolina in 1832 and in Louisiana in 1861, came to the state in 1837. Colonel Marshall acquired some 10,000 acres of rich Red River bottom lands and of the more healthful hill lands, the latter fertile enough to produce a bale and a half of cotton per acre. Here Marshall, one of the sixty-five slave owners in the United States who owned more than 300 slaves, built Land's End. Marshall's mother-in-law came with her daughter to Louisiana and complained that she had been "carried to the end of the earth," just a few miles from the Texas border. Hence the house completed in 1857 became "Land's End." It

was a two-and-one-half-story wooden house with set-back wings. The architectural builder was M. Robbins. The photograph has in the background one of the drawing-room mantels of Italian black marble. The wooden baseboards were in lifelike marble-ized finish. The wooden lower casement doors of the windows could be opened to the gallery and the tall windows then offered free ingress and egress.

LAND'S END: *Window Detail*

LASTRAPES
ST. LANDRY PARISH

In the south-central prairie lands near Opelousas, the forty-four-foot wide by thirty-nine-foot-deep Lastrapes house was built in the last decade of the eighteenth century. It was of low cottage design, T-shaped, of bousillage construction with plaster inside and out. Curiously, one exterior wall was of varied patterned brick. Three rooms had wooden baseboards and chair rails. There were one single and one double chimney, with brick hearths and wooden mantels. The doors, except the front one, were wooden batten with beautiful Spanish hammered-iron hardware. The front door was double hung and paneled to the door knob. The upper portions contained twenty-four panes of glass.

LASTRAPES: *Brick Panel*

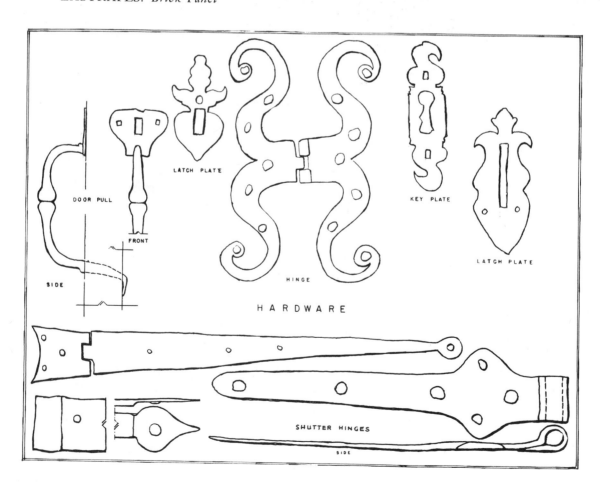

DOOR PULL

FRONT

SIDE

LATCH PLATE

HINGE

KEY PLATE

LATCH PLATE

H A R D W A R E

SHUTTER HINGES

SIDE

LASTRAPES: *Bousillage and Shutter Detail*

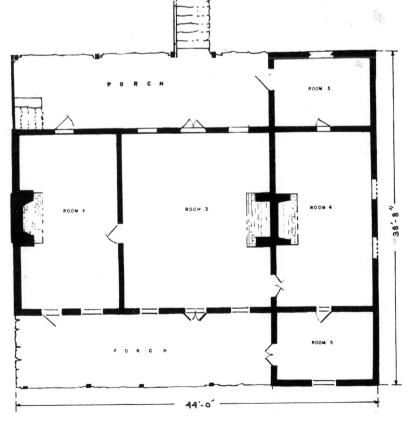

LASTRAPES: *Floor Plan*

113

LIVE OAK (ROSEDALE)
IBERVILLE PARISH

Andrew Jackson killed the father of Charles H. Dickinson in a pistol duel. In 1825 the younger Dickinson, grown and married, left Tennessee to select a plantation site in South Louisiana. He rowed for miles on flooded areas around Bayou Grosse Tête and found a small grove of live oaks above the water level. He erected a temporary log cabin and then his two-and-a-half-storied new home. It was from here that his widow built and managed a twenty-five-mile railroad before and after the Civil War. The house has many interesting features. The garage is a converted mellow red-brick plantation slave chapel. The front-window installations are unique. Narrow side lights are placed above paneling. The paneled shutters that fit into the recesses of the window casings formed by pilasters must have been the builder's own conception. When the shutters are closed they give privacy and allow a flow of air through the windows. When opened, they cover the side lights. The flint blocks and pilasters, the fluting and paneling, are as ornate as in many main doorways.

This post-Spanish Colonial home was built possibly before 1803 but more probably shortly thereafter. Its style is the well developed raised basement with a story and a half above. An outside stairway connects the lower and second galleries. One of the widespread Barrow clan, owners of Live Oak for a time, planted the live-oak alley in the early eighteen-thirties.

LIVE OAK
(ST. FRANCISVILLE)
WEST FELICIANA PARISH

Corner Fireplace

Enclosed Stairway

LIVE OAK (ST. FRANCISVILLE)

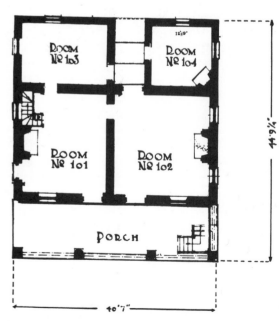

FIRST FLOOR PLAN

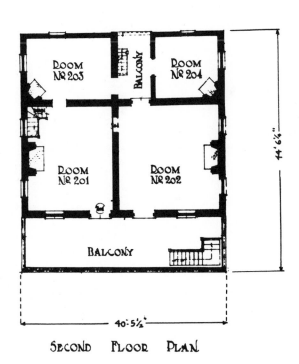

ROOM Nº 203   BALCONY   ROOM Nº 204

ROOM Nº 201   ROOM Nº 202

BALCONY

44′·6½″

40′·5½″

SECOND FLOOR PLAN

LIVE OAK (ST. FRANCISVILLE): *Interior*

The interior of Live Oak is very intriguing, suggesting more of New England in its plainness of trim and corner fireplaces. Within a few inches of a standard fireplace, a panel door conceals a sneak stairway which, as it reaches the upper floor, is enclosed simply by an open bannister. The eight medium-to-small rooms seem to belie the fact that the estate of one of its owners was valued at nearly half a million dollars.

117

LLOYD HALL

LLOYD HALL
RAPIDES PARISH

Located on the dividing line between sugar lands to the south and the hill lands of the central part of the state, this home reflects little that is characteristically Louisiana. It was built of slave-made bricks. The front wall was plastered and lined out in blocks. Tall square cypress columns spring from brick pillars to a high cornice unlike that of any other Louisiana plantation house. The front edges of the roofs of the galleries are higher than the backs, though not perceptible to the eye, in order to drain water to the center roof-line gutters. The high three-storied chimneys and the end brick wall may lend strength to the tradition that the house was erected in 1816 for one of the Lloyds of London. The ornate balustrades are of iron.

LLOYD HALL: *Plaster Decoration*

Lloyd Hall is in a fine state of preservation. All the original plaster cornices, center medallions, woodwork, floors and trim are practically as they were when the house was built. A broad hall runs through the center with the stairs hugging the hall to the third story, where a happy thought occurred to the builder. He opened a window upon the stairway for cross ventilation. Lloyd Hall was in the region of pine as well as cypress and oak, so slabs of heart pine were milled for enduring flooring. The eighteen-foot-high ceilings are the glory of its interior. In the first-floor hall medallions on each end flank a center medallion differing in pattern. Each plaster rosette of the various rooms differs from the others. This photograph of one of the drawing rooms indicates the lavishness of decorative detail.

The prolific Pughs of North Carolina transferred their slaves to the Bayou Lafourche region of Louisiana. Here among the Acadian Creoles they expanded and flourished and expanded again. The plantation remained in Pugh hands until 1916. Madewood was the product of the incredible riches that came from slave labor applied to as rich a land as the world knew. For four years Thomas Pugh cut, fashioned and cured his timbers, mostly cypress, and made his bricks, 60,000 or so. The title "Madewood" came naturally, with the house built essentially of the plantation's own wood. For four years construction was underway.

MADEWOOD
ASSUMPTION PARISH

In 1848 Thomas Pugh died and his widow partially completed the plans for the wings. The height of its entablature and pediment in relation to its width creates the effect of appealing loveliness. Six fluted Ionic columns rise from a low stylobate. On the inner side is attached a dainty, for this size house, shaped

balustrade for the second-floor gallery. The construction is particularly sturdy. The outside walls of brick, twenty-four inches thick, are plastered inside and out. The inner walls are eighteen inches thick. Interior trim, stairways, doors and mantels are all tastefully handled. Madewood has the customary large central hall, but in addition has side halls leading to the wings.

MADEWOOD: *Left Wing*

The wings are set back from the front of the house, matching their smaller gables with the central body. They have no columns, only heavy pilasters. Neither wing was completed according to the original plan. Thomas Pugh's widow did add a seventy-foot ballroom and service rooms to the left wing. The chimneys were enclosed to preserve the purity of line.

Thomas Ellis's 1858 home served as a "hospital," as did many Southern plantations located near scenes of fighting. In 1874 the home was renovated by the Shaffer family. The front is plastered brick. The remaining construction is of cypress. Magnolia has two and one-half stories with gabled ends. Squared split colonnettes with unmatched upper and lower balustrades give an effect which is disappointing. The interior of the house, with an impressive stairway, is much more attractive. A slave wash house still stands in the rear.

MAGNOLIA
(LITTLE BLACK BAYOU)
TERREBONNE PARISH

MAGNOLIA (LITTLE BLACK BAYOU):
Slave Bells

Thomas Ellis belonged to a large Mississippi and Louisiana plantation family. When
he built his southern Louisiana plantation home
in 1858 he provided a system to summon
household servants to the desired room. Call
bells were strung on the rear porch. Here they
still remain, amid the mud daubers' nests. On
the right the wires which ran to the various
rooms enter the walls.

MAGNOLIA (NATCHITOCHES PARISH): *Slave Cabin*

Just a few miles distant from the "traditional" site of Uncle Tom's Cabin there is a row of slave cabins facing Cane River. In the illustration cotton not yet in bloom grows to the very shadow of the "quarters." The taller wild-growing plant of the foreground is a botanical cousin of cotton, the prized okra — or gumbo to some farther north. The cabin with its coping on the end walls originally housed two complete families. A partition ran through the center with each half having its separate fireplace. The shed porch is a later

MAGNOLIA
NATCHITOCHES PARISH

addition. The "Big House" of the plantation was burned by General Banks, retreating after his attempt to capture Shreveport. Unlike other plantation owners whose homes were destroyed in this campaign, the Hertzogs, who owned Magnolia, immediately rebuilt on the same foundations.

Orange trees surround and touch the twenty-inch brick walls of Magnolia and extend to the ruins of the great sugar mill that gave it its greatest prosperity. The sturdy two-and-a-half-story home was built jointly by two sea captains, George Bradish and William M. Johnson, in 1795. Its ten rooms are large, approximating twenty-eight by twenty-two feet. After a century and a half of usage and neglect the house testifies to the durability of materials and quality of skills of the slaves who laboriously made brick, plaster, plank, panel, door, trim, window and frame that placed Magnolia as the first of the large homes between the Gulf of Mexico and New Orleans.

MAGNOLIA
PLAQUEMINES PARISH

In 1819 Benjamin Latrobe, the father of classical architecture in America, noted the house with approbation. All materials except the hardware were produced on the place. There are galleries front and rear, with now only an inside stair opening more from a central room than a hall.

MARY: *Rear*

MARY
PLAQUEMINES PARISH

Mary stands on the east bank of the Mississippi below New Orleans, in verdant semi-tropical lushness of growth. Here are Spanish daggers, palmettos, many varieties of fern moss, orchids and other air-borne plants, shrubs, citrus and many tropical fruits. Mary's late-eighteenth-century architecture is as one with its environment. The floor of the brick raised basement is at ground level. Ample windows and doors allow an unimpeded flow of cool moist Gulf breezes. Its verandas, running on all four sides, give abundant protection from the almost daily Gulf showers and the ever present hot sun. The high hipped roof has small dormers on two sides. The second floor, of mud-and-wood construction, while not ornate is particularly pleasing. The columns of the lower gallery are of concrete, made from molds with the wooden originals as patterns. The balusters are simple.

The village Waterproof has moved four times because of the Mississippi's raging waters. The last flood caused the removal of the McAlister plantation house to this northeastern village. The residence has a singularly high and wide gable roof with a modest front veranda. The west elevation shows a long downspout running from the front to back to supply cistern water. McAlister is known for an extra-large cast-iron breasted chimney front. A large decoration on the cast-iron

McALISTER
TENSAS PARISH

front served as a secret hiding place for money, jewels and documents when the house was repeatedly looted by Union soldiers.

The house called Melrose since the turn of the twentieth century was built by a wealthy free man of color, Augustin Metoyer, in 1833. He gave this house and plantation to a son Louis, and other properties to other children, all with slaves included. The census of 1840 shows that the Metoyers possessed the largest number of slaves owned by free Negroes in the United States. The house fortunately escaped the destruction that fell to so many in the neighborhood as General Banks retreated after his failure to capture the state capital, Shreveport. Melrose was not as pretentious as

MELROSE
NATCHITOCHES PARISH

other houses in the neighborhood, yet it is of considerable interest as being the largest now extant in this section which was built by

MELROSE: *African House*

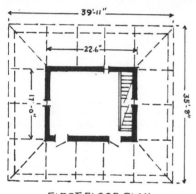

39'-11"

22'-6"

17'-0"

35'-8"

FIRST FLOOR PLAN

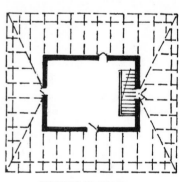

SECOND FLOOR PLAN

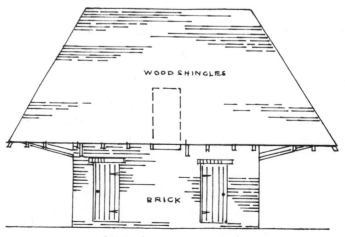

WOOD SHINGLES

BRICK

SOUTH (FRONT) ELEVATION

a free mulatto slaveholder. Augustin Metoyer gave land to establish a parish church for the mulattoes of Isle Brevelle. Even today in this section separate parochial schools are maintained for whites, Negroes and those who maintain the status of "children of strangers." Metoyer built the lower floor of brick, the upper of mud and moss packed between cypress posts. There were front and rear galleries, with a stair rising from each lower gallery. This photograph with its marked contrast of dark cool shade and brilliant Louisiana sunlight does not show the octagonal towers added by Mrs. Cammie Henry some fifty years ago.

MELROSE: *African House (opposite page)*

This unusual building was probably erected after Yucca and before Melrose. It has long been an unsolved puzzle to historians and architects. No other similar building exists in the United States. Its story-and-a-half brick center building is enveloped and made diminutive by the overhanging roof. The mushroom-beehive appearance strongly suggests a carry-over from the slave regions of West Africa. Its use was uncertain. Was it a plantation jail, or a storehouse? Today it is a museum; the wide eaves no longer provide shelter for farm wagons, trucks and implements.

MELROSE: *Yucca (below)*

Located on the same grounds are two interesting plantation homes established by free men of color. Yucca was without doubt colonial in origin. During the lifetime of Mrs. Cammie Henry it was used as a guest house for many well known literary figures, among them Lyle Saxon, who wrote so feelingly of Old Louisiana. A portion of the rear gallery of Yucca has been enclosed. Surrounded by banana, yucca plants and lush shrubbery, it stands as if its mud-between-posts construction would last another two centuries.

MOUNT AIREY: *Front Elevation*

MOUNT AIREY
ASCENSION PARISH

Some forty miles up the river from New Orleans, this choice wooden sugar-plantation home was erected just before the Civil War. It is raised, with the main floor surmounted by a hipped cypress-shingled roof, with extended ornate dormers having curved windows. The wooden columns are effectively individualized by their shape and capitals. The entablature is extensively carved and large for a house of this size. The interior is plastered. Mount Airey is one of the few plantation houses with much cast-iron ornamentation, which is also used on the belvedere.

MOUNT AIREY: *Rear Elevation*

Note the two ornamental cisterns which provided water for the household. These were essential either above or below ground until a few decades ago. Mount Airey was flanked by garçonnières and pigeonniers.

Situated about halfway between New Orleans and Baton Rouge, this house is said to have been built in 1836. The building has been recently "restored," to rescue it from its status as a hay barn. The raised-basement story-and-a-half home is of Louisiana style. It now has a wide lower hallway with the stairs running up to the attic rooms. The usual arrangement of two rooms on each side of the hall is followed. The mantels are of black marble, to complement the customary wide and thick plank floors.

MULBERRY GROVE
ASCENSION PARISH

134

This tastefully built small home with its classical portico and green shutters looks down from a De Soto Parish hilltop. Almost within "shouting distance" one can see three larger contemporary plantation houses, all built between 1840 and 1855. Edward Riggs planned Myrtle Hill for his intended bride, the daughter of the richest planter in the parish. She spurned him because she "had no inclination to struggle with heavy double hung windows without weights." He sold the house and died shortly thereafter, as legend has it, of a broken

MYRTLE HILL
DE SOTO PARISH

heart. A center hall is flanked by two rooms on each side, with a separate kitchen to the rear.

Built in the West Feliciana plantation center in 1833, The Myrtles has an elongated front elevation of 110 feet, with much elaborate cast-iron work. It is now so enclosed in deep shade from early morning to night that the exterior seems hazy the year round, favoring a "house ghost" legend. There are two room-size dormers, and others of more moderate size on the hipped roof. The home's chief interest is in the elaboration of plaster friezes, rosettes, choice woodworking, crystal chandeliers and antique furniture spilling over its dozen and a half rooms.

THE MYRTLES
WEST FELICIANA PARISH

NOTTAWAY
IBERVILLE PARISH

While Nottaway was built in Louisiana in 1857, there is little that is plantation Louisiana about this fifty-room mansion. John Hampden Randolph desired a residence distinctly different from those of other affluent Louisiana planters. Competitive drawings were submitted by New Orleans architects. Those of Henry Howard were chosen. His adaptations of classical modes produced some odd effects. Nottaway's columns, twenty-one in all, are tall and slender. The entablature with its brackets and heavy cornices is only in degree separated from the jigsaw styles of the Victorian period. The rounded and pillared ballroom wing was the first and last of its kind for a Louisiana plantation. Nottaway's reputed 200 windows were tall and restrained. Cast ironwork was used for balustrades. Inside, the rooms were large. There were expansive halls, six sets of stairways, a bathroom on each floor, huge water tanks on the roof, an all-white ballroom with white tiles and white-marble mantels. The entire construction project was indicative of the owner's desire to build a house that would surpass any other in the state. To Randolph's chagrin a near neighbor built Belle Grove, of pink brick to contrast with the white of Nottaway — and Belle Grove had seventy-five rooms. However, Belle Grove was razed by decay and fire, while Nottaway still stands.

Most Louisiana plantation homes were built and then landscaped, but not Bon Séjour, the house of good sojourn. The twenty-eight trees that form the alley were majestic giants in 1837-1839 when J. T. Roman replaced a lesser building. The architect Samuel Wilson, Jr., believes that builder George Swainey followed plans supplied by the architect Joseph Pilie, Roman's father-in-law. The trees of the alley were matched by the twenty-eight modified Doric columns to surround the classic façade of Bon Séjour. Each column supports the second-story gallery as it rises to a moderate cornice. The balustrades on the upper

OAK ALLEY
(BON SEJOUR)
ST. JAMES PARISH

gallery are of an individualistic stacked-grain design and are so proportioned that they could easily be mistaken for wrought ironwork. The matching balusters on the belvedere connect the tall chimneys, all harmonizing to create a sense of unity. The seventy-foot-square building is of slave-made brick and plastered in what is now a soft weathered pinkish tinge. A many-dormered attic story adds roominess to the nicely finished interior. One of the drawing rooms was originally floored with white marble to complement white-marble mantels. Oak Alley's chief charm stems not from its interior but from its exterior. Expansive landscaping surrounding each of its façades creates new entrancing ever changing frames.

OAK ALLEY (BON SÉJOUR): *The Alley*

The highway, and beyond it the Mississippi River levee, can be seen from the side gallery through the long vista of oaks. To stop on this road in a misty rain and view these mighty arched oaks is an experience never to be forgotten. Equally enchanting is the play of light and sunshine, ever changing with the movement of the sun, the clouds and the breeze, upon the green of the abandoned driveway, or upon creamy white columns, the herringboned brick of the lower gallery or the soft pinks of the walls. These trees lack the depressive atmosphere created by the ever present abundant growth of gray Spanish moss on the trees, bushes and even telephone

wires in the lowlands of the state. No moss is allowed in this nearly quarter-mile-long breathtaking arch. The term tunnel has been used by some observers, but tunnel seems to denote confinement. This is a great God-made outdoor nave, vaulting 200 feet in width. Each tree is some twenty feet in circumference five feet from the ground. Each is spaced forty feet apart and bids fair to grow larger and mightier as the centuries pass, if the capricious and voracious Mississippi permits.

OAK ALLEY (BON SÉJOUR): *Gallery Detail (opposite page)*

A tasteful Georgian touch is given the entrances on both floors. Double fluted columns rise to double caps, a headed shelf, and to a fan light. In the recessed curves are boxed panels. Green painted shutters hang by the tall plain windows with intricate small glassed transoms. Interior doors also are transomed. Potted banana plants are a minute sample of the larger plantings of the gardens.

The first half of the home, which at one time was called Oakland, was erected in 1832, in the Caddo Indian territory of northwestern Louisiana. Built of wood, its floors were two inches thick. On each end there was a brick chimney rising above a gabled story-and-a-half-high roof. There was a wide open hallway with rooms on either side. Back and front galleries ran the entire width of the house. An enclosed stairway ascended to the ample attic from the front gallery. In a separate building to the rear were the kitchen, the dining room and the nursery. In 1848 Dr. Abel Skannel erected a two-story building directly in front of the older one, converting the former front gallery to an open cross hall running the entire

OAKLAND
BOSSIER PARISH

width of the house. This simply constructed house was the headquarters for four other plantations, totaling over 8000 acres. Various legends exist about the house, one rising from the fact that the owner kept a handsome coffin in the attic. In the plantation cemetery Negro slaves and white master were buried side by side — unusual for a Southern plantation.

OAKLEY
WEST FELICIANA PARISH

When the building of Oakley began in 1808 the Spanish flag flew over West Florida, which included parts of Louisiana, Mississippi and Florida. The Florida parishes of Louisiana are hilly, with red sandy soil and running creeks. They differ greatly, even in vegetation, from the black low soils just a few miles away. Settled first by the English, 1763-1783, they attracted almost exclusively English, Scotch and American settlers. A Scotchman, James Pirrie, marrying the widow of Ruffin Gray, built upon the latter's 1770 land grant. Oakley today is a state historical memorial to James Audubon, who painted from this and neighboring plantations to produce his fabulous animal and bird series. Oakley has a raised basement, two stories and an attic. It is one and a half rooms deep and two wide, without a central hall. Double galleries run front and back. The lower gallery is supported by square brick columns rising flat from the ground. Turned colonnettes are used for the upper gallery. The roof is gabled, curving down to a plain cornice. Although Oakley was plenti-

143

fully shaded by a park of upland trees, extensive use was made of permanently fixed louvers. North Louisiana homes incorporated this same device. The stairway to the second floor mounts from inside the first floor gallery.

OAKLEY: *Dining Room*

In many Southern plantation homes the punka was a necessity if one wished to eat in comfort, and without the annoyance of flies. A young slave did the honors by gently pulling the cord. The mantelpieces on the main floor of Oakley are more elaborate than those of the lower. The many-paned windows are recessed. The baseboards are heavy. The total effect is one of restrained good taste.

OAKLEY: *Interior*

This fireplace of the raised basement reflected its heat on a bricked floor. The mantel itself was handcrafted, with vertical and horizontal fluting and paneling. Between the side door and the mantel, a small door opens into a warming oven. Such a device is an entirely unique feature in a Louisiana home. The attractive plain unpainted settle is an original possession of "restored" Oakley.

Near St. Joseph on the Mississippi with
its rich delta lands, Jack Watson acquired 3500
acres. He built a home facing Bayou Van
Buren around 1840. The Bayou gave him a
dependable waterway almost to the port of
St. Joseph. One hundred years later this writer,
after climbing from the raised-basement "slave
jail" to the attic, was told by a tenant occupant, "This is not much of a house, they didn't
know how to build in those days." Although
the house in recent years has had little care, it
was still sturdy and sound with its clapboards
and sills of non-rotting, termite-proof cypress.

ONEONTA
TENSAS PARISH

ONEONTA: *Rear Elevation*

In later years a three-room brick-and-
clapboard extension was added to replace the
original detached kitchen.

ORANGE GROVE: *Rear*

ORANGE GROVE
ST. BERNARD PARISH

Thomas Morgan, a railroad and steamship magnate as well as sugar planter, built his plantation in 1850 with only one concession to indigenous architectural adaptations. He erected a three-storied multi-gabled English manor house. Its Gothic pointed Tudor windows, high peaked gables and English-type chimneys were tempered only by modest galleries which have now disappeared. The interior contained the English "great hall," arched in the Gothic manner, with stained glass for the windows and transoms. The lower floors were tiled in varied colors. The main house contained sixteen large rooms with a rear wing of eight rooms for the household servants. Morgan used both marble and cast-iron mantels, the latter generally found only in plantations of northern Louisiana. He also had two other unusual features for this state, a real basement and hot running water.

ORMOND
ST. CHARLES PARISH

Ormond is Louisiana architecture without modification. Its central structure was built toward the end of the Spanish regime by Pierre Trepagnier. The fighting Butlers, as later owners of Ormond, replaced the original garçonnières about 1811. Under the probable supervision of the architect Henry S. Latrobe the two side wings were added. Here an even more indigenous and individualistic effect was achieved, for the two added wings were at a greater height than the center. Their galleries were connected. Ormond's shapes, outlines, both vertical and horizontal, and its subdued plastering have blended as the decades have passed. This 1940 photograph, with its plain honest weathered-cypress fence, its interim occupants, a Negro tenant's washing on the gallery, is used in place of a more modern illustration. Today Ormond glistens with new paint, sags have been removed, the lawn is trim, but it has a different savor. The sixty-foot front and rear walls are *briquette entre poteaux* lathed and plastered. The thirty-five-foot ends are of similar construction, except that mud (bousillage) is used instead of brick. The wings are constructed of plastered brick.

A portion of the front was lined off to resemble stone courses. Ten-foot galleries face the Mississippi River. It is thought that there were also rear galleries at one time. Short Tuscan-style plastered brick columns rise from low brick bases to the upper gallery, which is eleven feet from the ground level. Here squared cypress posts decrease in size at the balustrade railing and continue to a plain cornice. There are four rooms to each floor of the center, and two rooms to each floor of the wings. The enclosed passageways provide space for covered stairs.

ORMOND: *Detail, Door, Second Story Wing*

The half doors were wooden panels below and glass above. Two solid paneled shutters give in effect a double door. The fanlights and plastered ashlar courses are details of refinement.

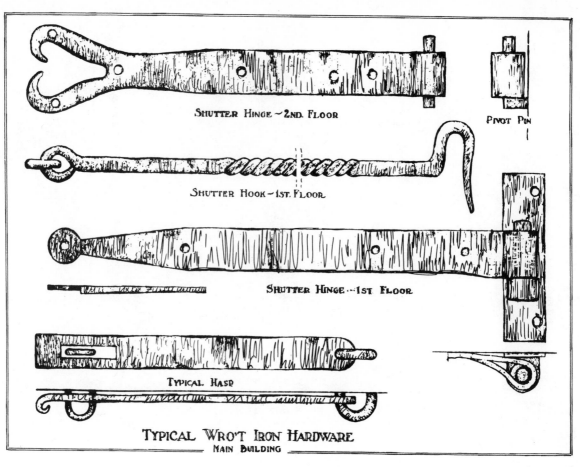

SHUTTER HINGE – 2ND. FLOOR

PIVOT PIN

SHUTTER HOOK – 1ST. FLOOR

SHUTTER HINGE – 1ST FLOOR

TYPICAL HASP

TYPICAL WRO'T IRON HARDWARE
Main Building

ORMOND: *Iron Hardware*

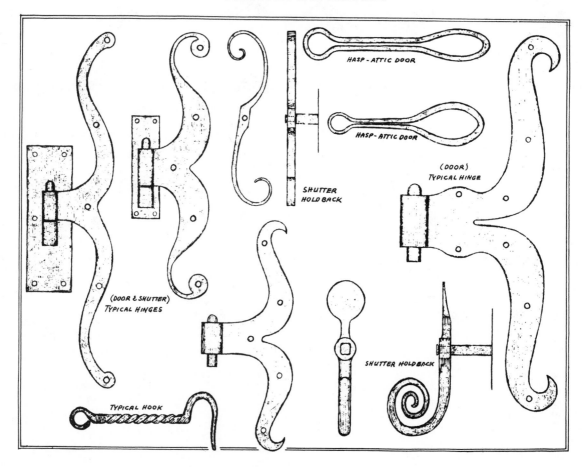

HASP – ATTIC DOOR

HASP – ATTIC DOOR

(DOOR)
TYPICAL HINGE

SHUTTER
HOLD BACK

(DOOR & SHUTTER)
TYPICAL HINGES

SHUTTER HOLDBACK

TYPICAL HOOK

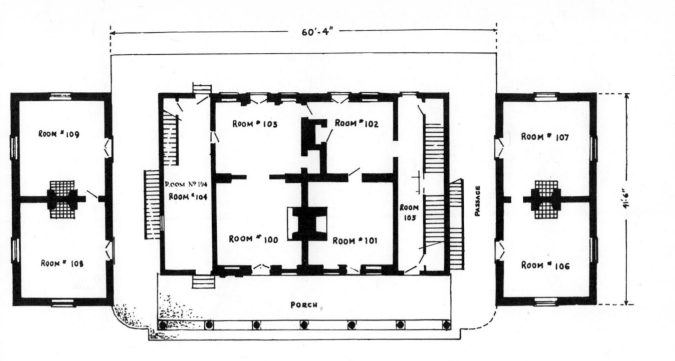

FIRST FLOOR PLAN

Room # 109
Room # 108
Room # 103
Room # 102
Room Nº 194
Room # 104
Room # 100
Room # 101
Room 105
PASSAGE
Room # 107
Room # 106
PORCH

60'-4"
41'-6"

ORMOND: *Floor Plans*

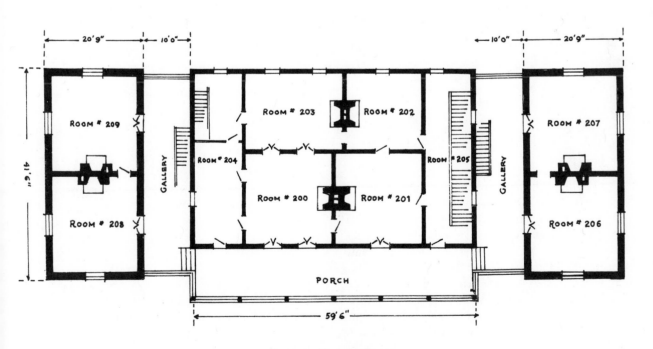

SECOND FLOOR PLAN

Room # 209
Room # 208
GALLERY
Room # 204
Room # 203
Room # 202
Room # 200
Room # 201
Room # 205
GALLERY
Room # 207
Room # 206
PORCH

20'9"
10'0"
10'0"
20'9"
41'6"
59'6"

151

PARLANGE: *Left Façade*

The Mississippi River, swinging southward in big lazy loops toward Baton Rouge, cut through one of the loops at the turn of the eighteenth century. The new oxbow lake formed in the old river bed became False River. Here, in Point Coupee Parish, the French made one of their earliest settlements. A French Marquis, Vincent de Ternant, received an extensive grant along the river, and in the decade before his death in 1757 built his home facing eastward towards False River. Parlange has not changed essentially in its life of over two centuries. The high dormered

hipped roof was extended to the rear sometime prior to 1860. A rear gallery was then added as before. It is thought that a stair mounted from inside the gallery rather than from the front, as it does today. Parlange is an excellent example of a raised-basement Louisiana Creole

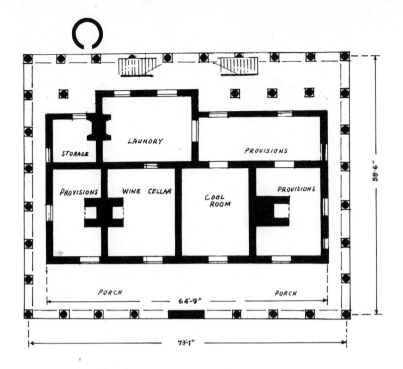

PARLANGE: *Ground Floor Plan*

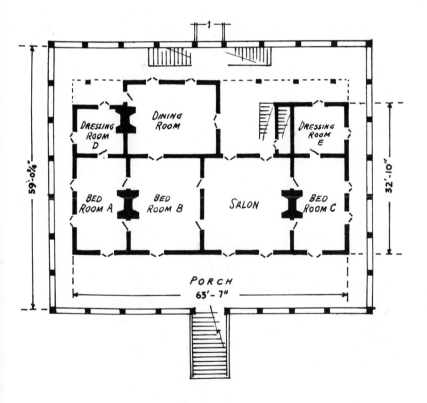

MAIN FLOOR PLAN

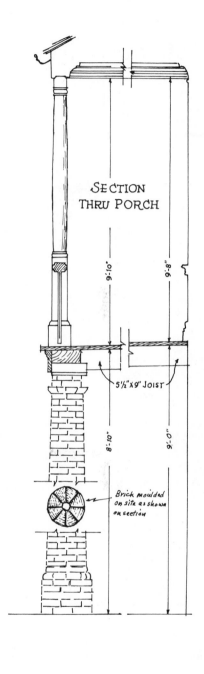

SECTION THRU PORCH

home. Built of brick below and plastered mud and cypress above, it has two large livable floors with higher ceilings than would normally be expected in a country house of this age. The short brick columns supporting the gallery are continued by cypress colonnettes. These are square to the height of balustrade railing and then taper to an inconspicuous cornice. There is no symmetrical placing of windows and colonettes, but the effect is pleasing.

PARLANGE: *Dining Room Mantel*

PARLANGE: *Interior and Sideboard*

The ceilings of the lower floor show sturdy beams. Those of the upper main level are of close fitting planks. The baseboards, wainscoting, cornices, doors, windows, trim and rosettes are all carefully made. Chimneys extend into each room. The mantelpieces, of plantation construction, are boxed and paneled on the sides. In the salon wooden Ionic columns support an arch on which the shelf rests. In the dining room the rounded columns support a panel of horizontal lines. Interior main-story doors are narrow, paneled and have false transoms.

PARLANGE: *Pigeonnier*

Halfway between the house and the lost iron decorative entrance gates stand two brick pigeonniers. From the highway running near the shore of False River their white brilliance lends piquancy to mossy trees amid what was at one time a formal French garden. The presence of these dovecotes, at most substantial early Creole plantations, is of course a direct transplantation from mother-country France.

PAYNE

ST. LANDRY PARISH

Payne was erected in 1857 by Dr. Archibald Webb near Washington, on the border of what at the time was prairie. This adjacent Bayou Courtableau and Bayou Boeuf could furnish transportation for the crops of the 4000-acre plantation. Wooden stairs, until recently double, mount to an extended landing. The stair railings are of wood, the gallery balustrade of iron. The lower story is brick, while wood is used for the principal floor. The front entrance door is glass side-lighted and opens into a broad hallway which runs to the back gallery. The gabled roof breaks to a new pitch at the inner gallery edge. The low cornice and thick round columns seem to tie the structure to the ground.

PAYNE: *Detail*

Spanish-type construction allowed for a carriageway through the very middle of the house. Subsidiary rooms were built on each side of the lower floor. Such is the case at Payne. Through the lower hallway a large sugar kettle can be seen. Such kettles are often found on southern Louisiana sugar plantations as relics of open-kettle sugar production. The principal bricked columns bell out as they reach the cornice, and invert at their bases. Curiously, the extension pillars for the stair landing have straight bottoms.

156

PLANT-MONTGOMERY HOUSE: *Detail*

In the hill lands of northwestern Louisiana, probably about the year 1850, the first of a series of log cabins was constructed. Later additions were connected to the adjacent cabin as they were built. One of these cabins was two stories in height. Today, with the exception of one room in the upper story, all logs have been completely concealed by milled lumber. Some ingenious craftsman contrived

PLANT-MONTGOMERY HOUSE
BOSSIER PARISH

disappearing sliding-door panels beneath the parlor's windows, thus making additional doorways.

NORTH ELEVATION

WEST ELEVATION

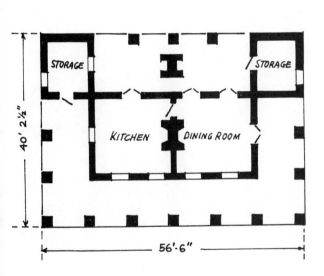

GROUND FLOOR PLAN

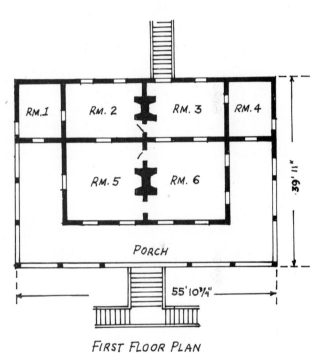

FIRST FLOOR PLAN

The Riche plantation, located in the False River section of Louisiana across the river from Saint Francisville, has become lost to historical records. Its chaste and refined lines show that it was a very old house of some pretension, reflecting the Spanish Creole influence with its very high hipped and dormered roof covering an area fifty-six by forty feet. It had seven short round columns across the front and two each on the half-length side galleries. Three columns gave a loggio effect in the central rear. The ground floor contained the dining room, kitchen and service rooms.

RICHE
POINTE COUPEE PARISH

The main floor had six rooms, with very choice mantels and trim. The upper gallery had turned colonnettes similar to those of Parlange.

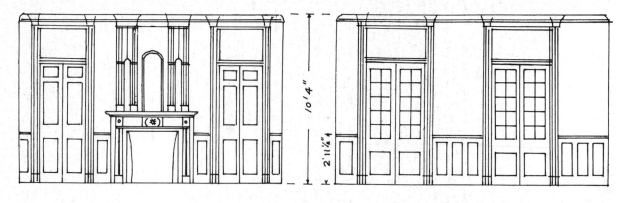

EAST ELEVATION   SOUTH ELEVATION

RICHE: *Mantel*

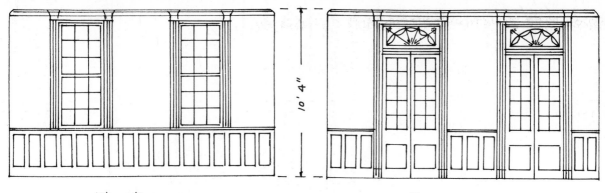

WEST ELEVATION   NORTH ELEVATION

ELEVATIONS OF ROOM 6

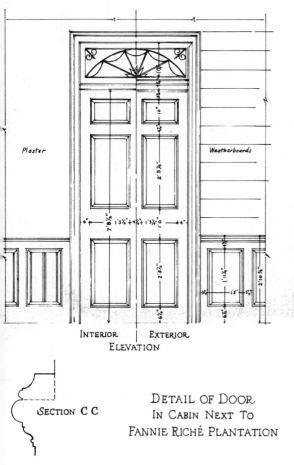

SECTION C C

DETAIL OF DOOR
IN CABIN NEXT TO
FANNIE RICHÉ PLANTATION

Cabin Next to Riche Plantation

This residence was probably built for a member of the family, as its interior walls were plastered and the details as carefully executed as in the Riche house.

161

RICHLAND
EAST FELICIANA PARISH

Slave labor constructed the thickly plastered brick walls of the 1820 bridal house of Elias Norwood. Located some forty miles north and east of Baton Rouge in the rich hill lands, it was recently acquired by the late Charles Wilson, former Secretary of Defense and former President of General Motors, and Mrs. Wilson. They remodeled the house. It also had been remodeled near the turn of the century. Many internal modifications of rooms were made, but still it is in harmony with the ante-bellum period. The exterior is relatively unchanged. The orginal house was carefully built, with four tall chimneys opening on each floor, each handsomely done. From a wide central hall a curving stairway runs upward. Trim and ceiling decorations have been re-

placed. At the turn of the century the once separated brick kitchen was joined to the main building. The exterior is not quite "typical" of Louisiana architecture; it seems more Eastern Seaboard in feeling. The bold end walls have one small Palladian opening. The portico is large, enhanced by four massive Doric plastered brick columns and a graceful entablature.

162

A romantic although implausible story credits the erection of this house by Queen Maria of Spain as a possible refuge from the disturbances of the French Revolution. The location chosen alone would have been highly unlikely. The house was built in the south-central part of the state near Bayou LaFourche and the present town of Thibodaux. The Spanish left behind examples of colonial residential architecture featuring a driveway through the central lower floor. Rienzi was originally so built. (The Payne house illustrates the only extant Louisiana plantation example though the Payne house has no Spanish relationship.) Rienzi's drive was brick enclosed in 1850. The house was not "fit for a queen," though at a distance, seen through the embracing arms of a live-oak tree, it is quite pleasing. Competent architectural observers have called Rienzi's architecture "crude." The house is shallow. The long renovated gables cover the two end half-galleries. The steps now seen are not original. The walls are thick and plastered. The interior is spacious, with irregular arrangement of rooms. Brick piers below and the wooden colonnettes, as well as the elaborate carvings of the interior woodwork, have been altered.

163

River Lake is a raised-basement Creole plantation home on False River near New Roads. It has a lofty hipped roof with dormers. A pair of square pigeonniers flanks the home in the front rather than the rear.

RIVER LAKE
POINTE COUPEE PARISH

When France decided in 1713 to place the first settlement in the Mississippi Valley, she chose the region of Natchitoches on the Red River. Ascending the Mississippi, the Red was the first river flowing out of the Spanish-claimed land to the west. To the first settlement of the future Louisiana Purchase there came a sprinkling of soldiers, merchants and planters with their slaves. Soon, just a few miles south of Natchitoches, the freed offspring of mésalliances with Negro slaves were living in a community known as Isle Brevelle. The Roque house, which is typical of the oldest construction in the state, has an interesting history. Locally known as the "priest's house" of a century ago, it also served as a "convent" until the yellow-fever epidemic of 1853. The gallery faces Cane River, which was the Red

ROQUE HOUSE
NATCHITOCHES PARISH

River when the house was built. Construction is of hewn squared cypress posts filled with mud and Spanish moss. The walls not protected by the gallery are covered by hand-split boards to protect the soft mud from the frequent hard Louisiana rains. The two half rooms on the back are undoubtedly a roughly executed enclosure of the back gallery. The hand-rived cypress shingles of the end gables, shining yellow brown in a setting sun, are a beautiful sight.

ROQUE HOUSE: *Interior*

A mulatto woman born in a large two-story Louisiana brick home spent more than three-quarters of a century of married life in this bedroom, rearing forty-five children, none of them her own. Until her death after the Second World War, she cooked in the fireplace, living a full, happy, useful and philosophical life. Her bedroom once had a brick floor but the bricks were removed by an occupant after the Civil War to build a "commercial" bake oven in the front yard. They were never replaced, The white areas of the rear wall are of mud which has been whitewashed. The whitewash has disappeared from the posts.

ROSEBANK

WEST FELICIANA PARISH

Don Juan O'Connor, later a Spanish al-
calde in the West Florida Parishes, built Rosebank. Various dates have been assigned as the
correct time of construction. After 1790 or
before 1808 would perhaps be correct. The
raised basement of brick supports an additional
story and a half. Short fat plastered brick columns support the gallery floor. The upper gallery originally had cypress colonnettes which
have been replaced by slender iron colonnettes, and wooden balustrades which have
given way to ornate ironwork. A brick ground
floor and an inside gallery stairway are typically Spanish. Rosebank, at one time known as
the Spanish Inn, has had a number of changes
made since the original construction.

ROSEDOWN: *Detail, Front Porch, Second Floor*

Daniel Turnbull and his wife, Martha Hilliard Barrow, built Rosedown in West Feliciana Parish near Saint Francisville. In the eastern productive hill lands about halfway between Natchez and Baton Rouge, it was several safe miles from the Mississippi. A local master builder started construction in 1834 and finished the main house in the following year. Ten years later two small Greek-mode wings with fluted Doric columns were added. In 1859 a back wing of no particular style gave more needed bedrooms. There were additional

ROSEDOWN
WEST FELICIANA PARISH

improvements: an expensive Greek Revival gateway was erected in 1845, and through two and a half decades changes and additions in the gardens were made. The summer-garden arbors so acclaimed by visitors for over a century took their chosen places. A pillared plantation office building went up in a proper setting.

The exterior of Rosedown's front façade is charming. There has been a haunting appeal of the interior rooms where each drape, each piece of furniture so widely and richly collected, has been maintained unmoved and unchanged by the Turnbull sisters and brothers for more than a hundred years, from the birth of the first child to the death of the last.

Surpassing all are the changing, changeless gardens. The author first visited Rosedown in 1929. Though time has altered the formality of the garden paths, the size of shrubs, the tidiness and extensiveness, the flavor still remains. The Turnbulls had seven levels in the garden crossed and divided by carefully planned alleys. Foreign as well as domestic sweet-smelling flowering shrubs, trees and flowers were grown with loving care.

The Turnbulls made wide use of statuary. A great stone urn at the front dooryard and

ROSEDOWN: *Entrance Doorway*

ROSEDOWN: *Garden Statues portraying (left to right) North America, Africa, Australia*

the large Carrara statues on brick plastered bases were judiciously arranged in symmetrically placed garden settings. One group was of the four seasons, another of classical mythology, a third of the six continents, all with a background of Spanish moss.

Rosedown was of composite architectural styles. The two-story cypress frame house used some local cedar. Its construction was reminiscent of the Tidewater houses of Maryland and Virginia, with Georgian windows and main door and trim. The plain Doric columns, made of home-cut cypress logs, supported the medium-sized entablature. All seems to have been in meticulous accord with the proportions set down in current builder's handbooks, with triglyphs and proper members present. Classic bulky balustration was used extensively. Pilasters were present on the classic wings. Some of the lumber was milled at Cincinnati and Philadelphia. A copper rainspout decorated with an American Eagle, dated 1835, was imported.

ROSENEATH
DE SOTO PARISH

William Bundy Means, of a prominent South Carolina family, came in 1844 to the fertile lands of North Louisiana between the Red River and the Texas border. He built the first large plantation house in the newly acquired Indian lands. His slaves made their crops and worked on construction of the house for three years. So carefully was their labor supervised that over a century later only one of the chimneys at the roof level has shifted one half of an inch. The semi-raised basement is of brick, the upper two stories of milled lumber. This Southern house shows few marked Louisiana characteristics, though its verandas are deep and its halls wide. Its gabled roof line is broken and widened on the front to accommodate the front gallery. Its balustraded verandas are protected on the first floor by jalousies, which are found in only a few north Louisiana homes.

ROSENEATH: *Drawing Room*

This plastered right drawing room has a black-marble mantel which was added some ten years after the house was built. A stylized wood trim is used throughout the house. This room is historic, for here the initiation ceremonies were performed for membership into the Knights of the White Camellia, a large law-and-order group widely confused with the Ku Klux Klan.

ROSENEATH: *Interior*

A rarity in an ante-bellum plantation home is the presence of two tremendous clothes closets. These are on the first floor, facing a twenty-foot hallway.

ROUBIEU HOUSE
NATCHITOCHES PARISH

In 1808, five years after the Louisiana Purchase, François Roubieu, a Frenchman, built on Isle Brevelle. One of the first white men to build in this vicinity, Roubieu made his home much larger and more substantial than those of the neighboring free men of color. The house stands today essentially the same as when it was built. The back gallery and outbuildings are gone, paint has been absent for years, but it is as sturdy as ever. To the left rear of the house are located two huge dome-shaped underground cisterns. Until recently these were covered by a large, substantial building. Many of the old plantations had underground brick cisterns but none had such a large multipurpose enclosure. The house itself is a raised-basement type with a heavy brick plastered wall below, with mud and moss between posts above, covered with cypress siding. The hipped roof is dormered. The rooms are large. The writer saw five double beds "comfortably" placed in one room. On the upper gallery there are four door openings whose only closure consists of paneled shutters; each opening has a fixed glass transom. There is only one glass window, which has louvered shutters. The unusual location of doors and window is entirely unique. Fifteen-feet-long columns were found in the attic but it is not believed that this house ever had a different appearance, except perhaps for the outside stairs. Chimneys are interbuilt through the inner walls and extend into the rooms. They are encased in large boxed paneling from floor to ceiling.

Certainly not clearly akin to other Louisiana plantation homes, San Francisco's eclectic architecture needs "classification." Perhaps "Steamboat Gothic" is a misnomer; the house is said to have resembled the superstructure of the daily passing steamboats. The over-all aspect is somewhat oriental. The general line is horizontal rather than Gothic, except in the original meaning of the term as being barbaric (different) and nonclassical. There is much ornamental gingerbread. The few arches that are used inside and out are flat and shallow. San Francisco is certainly an interesting house, nestling as it does within a few hundred feet of the Mississippi River, with the levee and

SAN FRANCISCO
ST. JOHN THE BAPTIST PARISH

road squeezed in between. Its weathered front seems more appealing than its other façades, which are screened by the omnipresent gray moss hanging from the trees. The owner is said to have remarked when he finished construction in 1850, "Son saint-frusquin" ("I have lost my all"). This phrase, anglicized into San

Francisco, came into usage. The house is built of plastered brick with galleries which run across the front and part of the way down the sides. Cast iron, said to have been imported from France, is blandly intermixed with wood. Square brick pillars are used below to support the gallery; above, fluted Corinthian columns of wood are used with cast-iron capitals. These meet flat arches which in turn support a balustraded narrow "deck" from which an immense entablature is evolved. It is easy to understand that San Francisco was planned to be different. The double outside stairway has a wooden balustrade; the gallery balustrade is of cast iron, of a different pattern. The balustrade

design of the "deck" is again changed. Much that was done seems incompatible with other parts, yet all in all, it is very pleasing. The hipped dormered roof is surmounted by a low belvedere with small windows. Fortunately the present owners had the taste and foresight to replace the roof with the same type of slates originally used. A huge wooden cistern stands on the right.

SAN FRANCISCO: *Interior (Salon)*

Just as San Francisco is unique externally, so also is there an interior individualism, especially on the main floor. Here iron posts en-

176

tirely encased in wood, with cast-iron capitals, masquerade as classical columns. The iron capitals are similar to those used by north Louisiana De Soto Parish builders for outside columns. In this illustration iron capitals can be seen supporting deep ceiling beams. An Italian painter, Dominique Canova, painted frescoes and ceilings of different patterns, and originally there were designs on large folding doors and the walls of some of the rooms. The house contains none of the original furniture or china but is now overflowing with genuine, carefully selected collections of museum pieces of silverware, furniture, china and other household furnishings.

SAN FRANCISCO: *Bedroom*

The cradle is thought to date back to the Tudor period. Solidly made of English oak, it is beautifully carved and executed.

Now in the industrial area of New Orleans, Seven Oaks stands abandoned and doomed. Built around 1840 by a descendant of Johan Zweig, a 1724 German immigrant whose name had been latinized into La Branche, the house was named for the live-oak trees that surrounded it. Built of brick, plastered with eighteen plainly ornamented rooms, it is reputed to have been designed by Valentine von Werner. Square and enduring, the twenty-eight simple Doric shafts support a second-story gallery that completely surrounds the

SEVEN OAKS
JEFFERSON PARISH

house. The functional balustrading matches the mood of the house, strength and simplicity. Only the belvedere above the dormered roof seems out of harmony, and this may have been a later addition.

Recently restored by the National Trust for Historic Preservation, this plantation house of the Weeks family is now most carefully preserved. David Weeks's father, an Englishman who received his first land grant from the Spanish in 1792, as was the custom with many planters, operated a number of plantations. In 1825 David acquired a site on the lovely placid Bayou Teche, which is now in the town of New Iberia. In 1831 he employed James Bedell, a master builder, to start construction of The Shadows, which was com-

SHADOWS-ON-THE-TECHE

IBERIA PARISH

pleted in 1835. The Shadows has been gathering beauty ever since. As the family fortunes declined after the Civil War, the bricks lost their white paint, the walls became a natural shade of salmon pink, set in a landscaped gar-

den that became very small as the town grew. Its exterior architectural beauty surpassed that of the interior, which was plainly handled. The house is of moderate size but its proportions and setting create a sense of harmony. Three tasteful dormers are in each side of the gabled roof, which covers front galleries on two levels and a central loggia in the rear. Eight pleasing brick-and-plaster Doric columns rise to the front from oversize bases to a moderate entablature including a frieze with highly individualistic triglyphs.

The interior of the house follows the favorite Creole arrangement of three rooms across the front and two deep, with no interior halls. There is one modest interior sneak stair, to complement the outside front-gallery stairway. In the background there has always been the Teche and verdant growth. Some compare The Shadows architecturally with Chretien Point, but it is difficult for a layman to feel any sense of similar savor, for Chretien Point is interiorly more sophisticated.

SHADOWS-ON-THE-TECHE: *Dining Room (opposite page)*

Very similar to the one in the drawing room, the chandelier is more ornate and probably of later origin than others in the house. The dining room is furnished with Hepplewhite and Sheraton pieces and is floored with contrasting colored tile, a Creole practice adopted by this English plantation owner. The sideboard and dining table are of moderate scale, with a seating capacity of eighteen people. The flatware is French vermiel, and has long been a family heirloom.

180

SHADOWS-ON-THE-TECHE:
Drawing Room

This charming room has a fourteen-inch-wide cornice, a hurricane lamp on an Empire table, a pre-Civil War rosewood Pleyel piano with Confederate music, a wooden carved mantel with fenders, logs and fire tenders, a pair of whale-oil lamps, a Sheraton card table and period chairs. The heavy Empire side table contrasts with the delicacy of the room's other furniture.

SHADOWS-ON-THE-TECHE:
Back Bedroom

American Sheraton, Chippendale and New
Orleans Creole furniture furnishes this back
bedroom. Here the original owner's pants are
on display (although not shown in picture).
Worn by a high-waisted seven-foot-and-one-
inch-tall-man, they would cover an average
person from nose to foot.

SHADOWS-ON-THE-TECHE:
Front Bedroom (below)

The high-canopied four-poster bed needs
steps for one to get into it. At the foot of the
bed there is a large revolving rail, from which
a rolled blanket could be pulled. The Empire
chairs seem dainty in contrast to the large day
bed.

SHADOWS-ON-THE-TECHE: *Bedroom Detail*

The dainty full tester bed with mosquito netting pulled back reveals the dress worn by a daughter of the house in the oval picture painted in 1859. The tin bathtub was commonly used. The dresser has china pieces to hold a man's cuff links and watch. The armoire was conveniently placed.

The Erwin family from Tennessee spread a network of plantations that threatened to rival the Bringier and Barrow enterprises. Isaac Erwin erected Shady Grove a few years before the Civil War. Built of brick, the house tended to narrowness. The front portico, two stories high, appeared as an unnatural projection, tied to the house by a generous dentiled entablature. The columns of the portico were Ionic below the Corinthian above. The windows were unusual.

SHADY GROVE
IBERVILLE PARISH

Before 1730 the first construction was begun on what is now more than a modest Creole plantation house. Two rooms wide, one deep, it rose two stories, with verandas across the front and back and an exterior stairway. All additions, with the exception of a music room in the rear and dormers, are thought to have been completed by 1784. The lower floor is of plastered brick with heavy masonry pillars. Rounded wood colonettes support the slight cornice. The second story is of wood. The roof is hipped and now dormered. Porch and ceiling rafters are left exposed. The house is handcrafted, including its old Spanish wrought-

SPANISH CUSTOM HOUSE
ORLEANS PARISH

iron hinges. Since it is located on Bayou St. John, a natural highway for both honest trading and smuggling between the lakes and New Orleans, this house acquired its name by its use as a custom-inspection station under the Spanish regime.

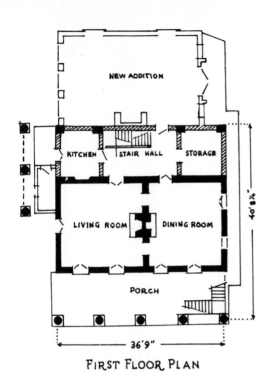

FIRST FLOOR PLAN

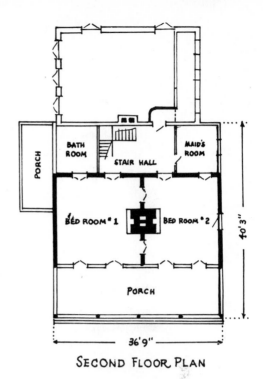

SECOND FLOOR PLAN

SPANISH CUSTOM HOUSE

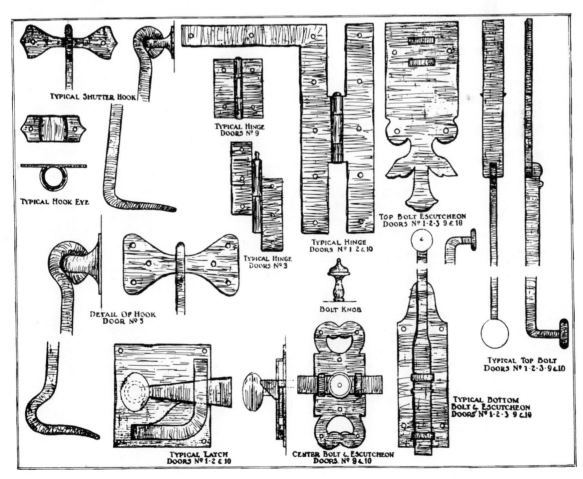

SPANISH CUSTOM HOUSE: *Cornice and Mantel Detail*

STAR ARLINGTON
EAST CARROLL PARISH

Lake Providence lies along the Mississippi not far from the Arkansas line. From here U. S. Grant's generals tried to move down overland on the western bank during the Vicksburg campaign. Nearby Arlington, as did many plantation homes, served as a staff headquarters. Three Union generals quartered here were later to return and purchase adjoining plantations. Arlington was fortunate not to have been burned, as were many other houses in this region. Mrs. T. R. Patten built the first four large rooms in 1841. Edward Sparrow, a native of Ireland, had a modest plantation at Vidalia across the river from Natchez, named Sparrow's Nest. Profits from this plantation enabled him to purchase Arlington in 1852. Sparrow raised the wooden building of Mrs. Patten and erected a new floor underneath. Its lower brick columns are not quite aligned with the fluted ones above. All columns have plain capitals. The gallery extends across the front and part of the way down one side. The principal entrance, with a fanlight and side lights, is on the second floor but there are no stairs leading to it. The balustrade topping the bracketed cornice is of a more intricate pattern than that of the gallery below. Arlington's interior is not as ornate as the exterior.

Three Oaks is now maintained on the grounds of the American Sugar Refinery in New Orleans. It is surrounded by live oaks, palms and cedar trees. It seems as pristine as when it was built in 1840. Large plastered-brick Doric columns rise from a stylobate on all sides to a plain entablature which is topped by a hipped roof. Two dormers face the river, and there is one on each side. The wooden balustrade on the upper gallery is in keeping with the somewhat severe though individualistic trim of the interior.

THREE OAKS
ST. BERNARD PARISH

190

Said to have been built in the early 1800's, this most unusual, almost whimsical, plantation home on the river road south of Baton Rouge is made of plastered brick. There are two balustraded galleries with small wooden columns which are dwarfed by a pair of turrets with peaked roofs. The remainder of the house seems to seek oblivion. The low hipped roof with its single dormer is almost invisible because of the high entablature with its primitive scalloped pattern.

ZENON TRUDEAU HOUSE
ST. JAMES PARISH

The most extensive, the best executed and perhaps the most beautiful ante-bellum plantation complex in Louisiana was that of Pierre Auguste Samuel Fagot, Uncle Sam, about halfway down the river between Baton Rouge and New Orleans. There were certainly other plantation houses which excelled the main house, but none could compete with Uncle Sam's composite grandeur. It was a national loss when workmen, blasting and tearing at the solid structure for salvage, had to abandon the site to the surging waters of the changing Mississippi River. Samuel Fagot, a native of La Rochelle, France, had acquaintances among the Tureauds and Bringiers, and to them he came in 1828. An independent man, he began growing sugar cane on a small scale. He was close-mouthed and acutely able. He accumulated wealth and more wealth, all the while planning

UNCLE SAM
ST. JAMES PARISH

an estate, not piece by piece but as an integrated whole. Steadily Fagot accumulated and cured his wood and brick. After each sugar grinding his slaves continued the seemingly endless tasks. Then one year brick foundations were laid according to the predetermined master plan. He did not hurry. He built steadily and sturdily. By 1849 he was ready. Columns sprouted. Twenty-eight giant shafts went around the two-storied main house, and six at the front and six at the rear of the flanking

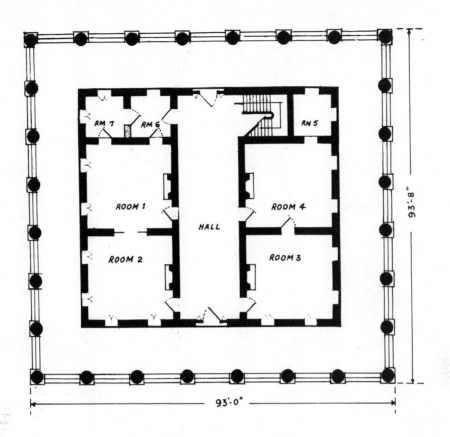

UNCLE SAM: *First Floor Plan*

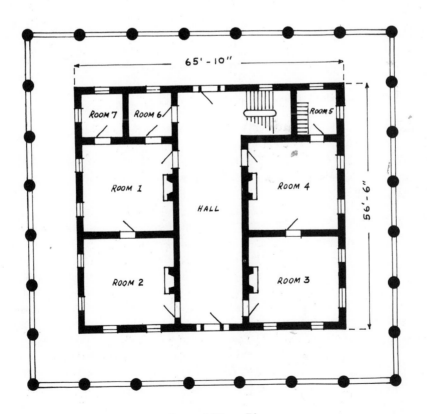

Second Floor Plan

193

UNCLE SAM: *Garçonnière (left) and Main House*

garçonnières. There were four more each for the fronts and four for the backs of the business office and the kitchen. They totaled fifty-six columns. Fagot's main house was ninety-three feet square. Of this twelve feet and two inches were taken by the verandas which encircled the house. The central halls were sixteen feet wide and over fifty-six feet in length. A stairwell turned off the rear of each hall, running to the attic. There were four large and three smaller rooms to each floor. The original interior finish was plaster, as were the cornices. The original hearths and mantels were of brick and wood. At a later stage cast-iron grates and marble mantels were installed. Wide thick cypress boards provided the flooring. The other buildings were restrained in their interior finishings. The plastering inside and out, due to the river sand used, was of a brownish tinge that held its color through the decades that followed.

Recessed sufficiently to the right and left of the main house, from the river one could see the column fronts of the office and the kitchen, and the garçonnières. The latter were sixty-five and a half feet wide and forty-five and a half feet deep. There were two nineteen-foot, ten-inch by sixteen-foot, ten-inch rooms, a hall and two "smaller" rooms. To the sides and rear were identical pigeonniers, thirty-five feet from the ground to their finials. Their lower floors served useful purposes.

Behind the pigeonniers were formal gardens and orchards. Further to the rear were a large sugar mill, the blacksmithy, the stables, the commissary, the hospital and the slave quarters, making forty-six buildings in all. The omnipresent cisterns were situated where needed. Three double live-oak alleys led to the main buildings, and a single row of trees marked the boundary of the home complex.

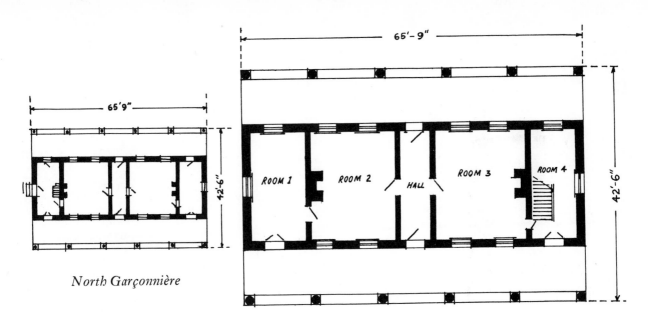

North Garçonnière

UNCLE SAM: *South Garçonnière*

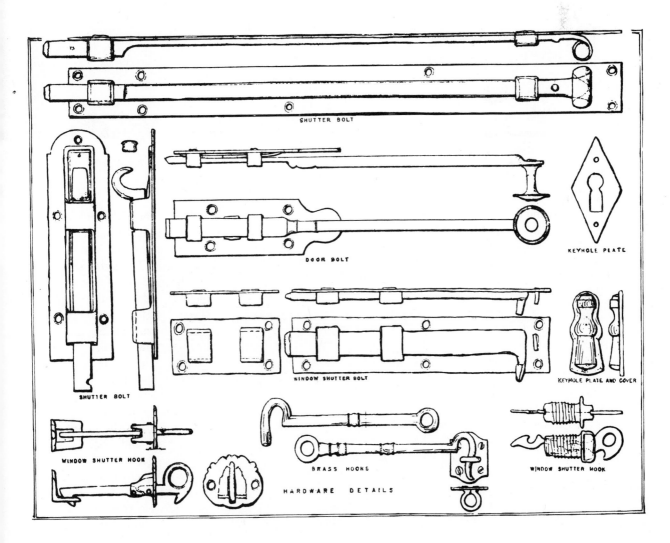

HARDWARE DETAILS

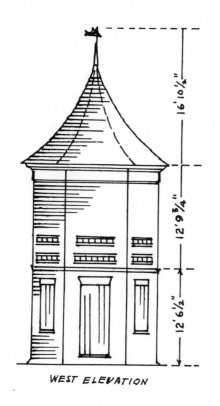

NORTH PIGEONNIER

SECOND FLOOR PLAN

FIRST FLOOR PLAN

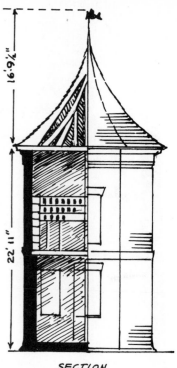

WEST ELEVATION

SECTION

UNCLE SAM

196

UNCLE SAM: *North Office and Pigeonnier*

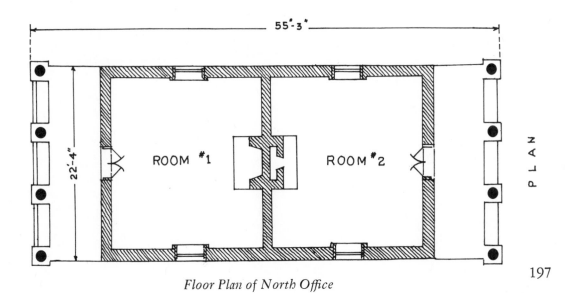

Floor Plan of North Office

Waverly, built in 1821, is located on the eastern side of the Mississippi north of Baton Rouge. Nestling beneath high-growing trees after a long period of neglect, it has not lost the delicacy of its Georgian style, which did not appeal to the following generation of lush plantation expansion. There are lightness and grace in its proportions, both in its exterior and interior. The house is all of wood, made mostly of cypress except the laths, which were of walnut under the plastering. The pure Georgian doors, side lights, fan lights and

WAVERLEY
WEST FELICIANA PARISH

trim of careful workmanship, with smoothness of window, of baseboards and chair rails that blend with the choice Adam mantels, make the first floor most attractive. One feature of this home is built-in clothes closets and built-in cupboards. The mahogany stair rail is nicely executed.

198

Elam Bowman's parents fled from Ireland in 1777 and he was born in New Madrid, Missouri, in 1804. Living near St. Francisville, he lost his first wife when she drowned crossing the Mississippi to attend church. He married again in 1839. In 1840 he bought 3200 acres of land in Tensas Parish. Later, with his own money and some of his wife's, he bought 1500 acres more. Much of his land was covered by growths of native pecans, cedar, cypress, elm, hackberry, ash and several varieties of oaks. At one time he had 800 acres deadening. He built or occupied a modest home on the new lands which he later incorporated into his newer and more expansive mansion, Wavertree. Bowman put his slaves to making cotton. In their spare time they were hewing incredibly sized red-cypress timbers. These were seasoned for a minimum of three years by wrapping them in oiled burlap. With bricks, heavy timbers and painfully "hog sawed lumber" available, Bowman was ready to make a trip to St. Louis. There he bought $50,000

worth of slaves, a $12,000 steamboat and some hardware. Docking his steamboat near his plantation, he loaded it with several years' accumulation of cotton and steamed to New Orleans, where he sold the boat and the cotton at a profit. Returning to Tensas Parish, he had an argument with S. Essleman, the architect he had engaged from New York. Essleman wanted to incorporate clothes closets, but Bowman would have none of this newfangled nonsense and dismissed him. Bowman had made other preparations for building when he purchased skilled slave mechanics in St. Louis. One of these, Christopher Caleb, cost some $2500 and was responsible for Wavertree's fine paneling, wainscoting, doors and trim. Every-

thing that went into the house, with the exception of hardware, marble mantels and the walnut stair railings were produced on the plantation. The house was large. Twelve times around the gallery, and the owner had had his one-mile morning walk. The size of the timbers used is unequalled in any other house in the state. Some of the roof rafters are seventy feet long and over two feet square. Bowman intended these to hold level the heavy slates he had ordered from Europe. When the war prevented the shipment of the slates, cypress shingles were substituted. Wavertree's cornice is plain, the chimneys enclosed and the hipped roof surmounted by a railed belvedere. The outside walls and ceiling of the galleries were plastered. The walls simulated genuine veined marble.

WAVERTREE: *Interior*

Elam Bowman was riding the crest in 1860. Despite the diversion of labor forces to the building of Wavertree, he had produced some 1500 bales of cotton. He ordered slate, plaster medallions and cornices, marble mantels, and silver door knobs and hinges from Europe. Furniture, the exact duplicate of his sister-in-law's home, Rosalie, in Natchez, Mississippi, was ordered from New York. But the Civil War came. Cypress shingles were the only major outside substitute, but inside there were no medallions, no cornices, as the raw scratch plaster of the drawing room illustrated so mutely testifies. No new furniture — only the silvered hinges and marble mantels arrived ahead of the Union blockade.

Front

Colonel Charles P. Edwards left South Carolina and came to northwest Louisiana in 1835, just as the United States was purchasing land and removing the Caddo Indians. He urged his friends to migrate and a number of large slave owners did so. Whether because the Texas and Mexican problems made him cautious, or for other reasons, Edwards did not begin building Welcome Hall until 1851, finishing the central portion in 1853, the first wing in 1855, and the second in 1857. Robbins, the master contractor builder whose business procedures have elsewhere been discussed, was given free reign to design and build. Robbins had a penchant for large brick piers from which he carried his forty-four columns to an entablature which has a horizontal beaded molding topped with dentils. Independent

WELCOME HALL
DE SOTO PARISH

piers, almost columns in themselves, carried the weight of the wings. The window glass came from France and the wrought ironwork from England or France. All of the rear balustrades were tastefully constructed of wood by Robbins himself, without the use of nails, as he did in the building of Buena Vista. There were eleven rooms, ten large fireplaces, and four bathrooms without plumbing. The two wings were connected to the main house by a continuous U-shaped gallery. The main entrance was very beautifully pedimented.

Rear

WHITNEY: *Rear Gallery*

WHITNEY

Whitney was built on the river some miles above New Orleans during the last years of the Spanish Colonial period. Constructed of bousillage, the raised-basement home had a Greek Revival front added after 1840. Whitney was nicely finished, having a hipped roof with dormers in the front. The walls of the front and rear galleries were marbleized and ornately decorated. Interior walls were painted as one would paint Dresden china. The wrought

Spanish hardware was heavily scrolled. The rear gallery, supported by fat round brick plastered columns, was enclosed by extensive stationary jalousies.

WINTER QUARTERS
TENSAS PARISH

Haller Nutt has left an architectural impression on the hundreds of thousands who have made the Natchez, Mississippi, pilgrimage and viewed the unfinished "Nutt's Folly," named Longwood, under construction when the Civil War came. Nutt and other Louisiana lowland planters left their fever-ridden plantations during the summer and spent several months in their Natchez mansions. One of Nutt's Louisiana plantations quite naturally took the name "Winter Quarters." Local tradition declares the name Winter Quarters was used because Grant "spent the winter there in his Vicksburg operations." Grant may have spent a few days there in the spring of 1863, but legal records show the name was used years before the war. Nutt acquired his property partially from his wife, who was related to the rich Routh and Bowie (of the fabled knife) families, and by purchase. In 1857 he bought from John Routh 1718 acres for $175,000. At his death in 1861 he owned 3300 acres of land in Louisiana. The house has been enlarged from its original size at least twice,

as indicated by the set-back gallery and construction not shown. There are useable rooms in the attic. The house was built on brick piers, of steam-milled lumber.

WOODLAND: *Slave Quarters*

The two sea captains who built Magnolia on the Mississippi River in 1795 quarreled. Bradish Johnson then established Woodland, just four miles upstream. There are four two-story brick buildings of the slave quarters still standing. (Two-story brick slave quarters were unusual in Louisiana.) With four rooms to a building, they probably housed seventy-five field hands. Two of these buildings are still inhabited. The gardens around them are harvested twelve months of the year.

WOODLAWN
ASSUMPTION PARISH

In Assumption Parish, on each bank of Bayou Lafourche, "the longest little street in the world," there are small "cajun" houses within hailing distance of each other. The bayou is no longer the street, for on each bank there is now a paved road, yet on Sundays one can see boatloads of parishioners converging for mass at the nearest church.

There were only two non-French families in the region when the Pughs arrived from North Carolina in 1818. They began to populate the region as well as extract fortunes from the rich cotton and sugar lands. To a favorite Creole conundrum, "Why is Bayou Lafourche like an aisle in the church?" the answer was: "Because there are Pughs on each side." William W. Pugh erected the first large Pugh

home. There is no evidence of an architect, although certainly skill and experience directed the purchase and fabrication of plantation building materials over a period of several years. With only the one-story wings being pedimented, the absence of dormers in the gabled roof, and the heavy line of the entablature with an unique rising parapet, all seemed to affiliate the house with the low land mass

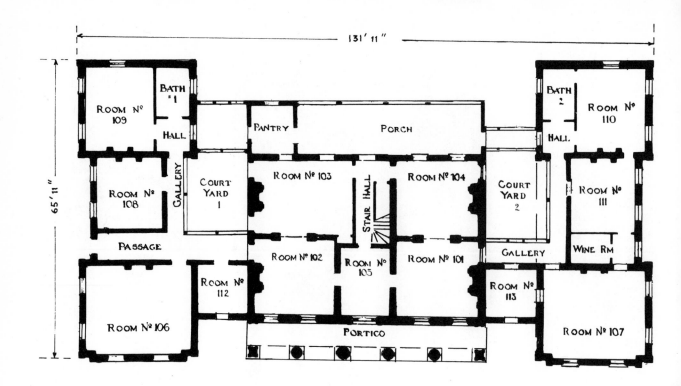

FIRST FLOOR PLAN

WOODLAWN

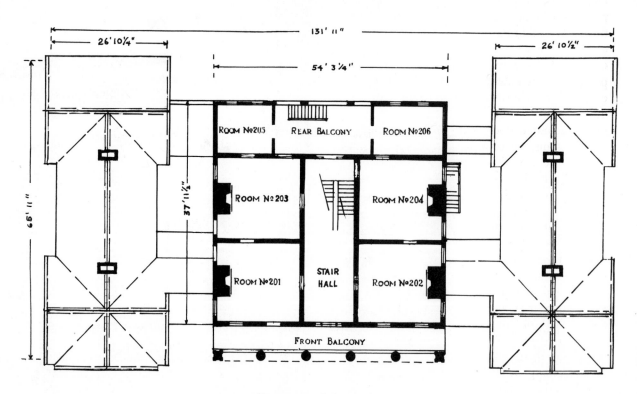

SECOND FLOOR PLAN

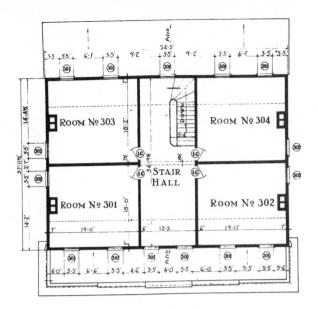

THIRD FLOOR PLAN
Scale ⅛″=1′-0″

of the fields. Great heavy square plain columns rose to a flat cap on each end of the gallery, the four Ionic columns between with great white marble capitals. This is the only known use of marble capitals of such size in Louisiana plantation homes. The wings and entire first floor were of brick while the upper portions of the house were of clapboard, with the exception of the front façade, which was heavy plaster over wooden laths. The first-floor façade and the wings were plastered with a more durable finish. The central entrance had elaborate decorated doors with leaded side lights and transoms. There were six rooms of various sizes on the main floor and a relatively modest rear hallways and stairwell. The second story had six rooms with a thirty-six-by-twelve-foot central hall, and a stairway to the top floor. The top floor had four rooms, with only one window to each room and slanted ceilings. The special feature of the house was two inner courtyard areas which were surrounded by narrow galleries protected from the weather by permanent jalousies. Each wing had a bathroom, one for the great marble block later taken to Afton Villa. The interior of Woodlawn had plastered walls and cornices with center ceiling decorations.

Woodlawn no longer exists.

WOODLAWN: *Detail of Window Trim*